The Woman in the Middle

A Guide to a Woman's Treasure.... Her Mind

By M.J. Rachal

DORRANCE PUBLISHING CO
EST. 1920
PITTSBURGH, PENNSYLVANIA 15238

Dorrance Publishing Co
585 Alpha Drive
Pittsburgh, PA 15238
Visit our website at *www.dorrancebookstore.com*

ISBN: 979-8-88812-121-4
eISBN: 979-8-88812-621-9

"For those who only felt alone
because they never knew me."

Table of Contents
"The Woman in the Middle"

I.

Why Did I Even Write this Book?

So, I have to start out first by saying, no, I am not an expert. I didn't go to school for this, never taught a class for this, or even been with or around a large enough number of women to even really prove a legitimate point to what this book even portrays or tries to defend. This is a simple observation coming from a guy who's had a pretty unusual array of "relationships"/encounters with the fairer sex. So unusual, in fact, that I felt so compelled to write this book just for the sure thought that I needed some type of confirmation or co-sign from other men that can relate to anything pertaining to these stories and descriptions. So that instead of me feeling I've sustained weird and unexplainable situations with women, I instead can see it's actually quite normal. Knowing actually would give me some type of peace and reassurance that would allow me to sleep well at night.

Now before I can even demonstrate the reasoning of why I also felt this book was necessary to write besides my own personal mindset, allow me to give my thoughts to this little memoir and lessons credibility by saying first and foremost, I do not talk about the exception pertaining to the types of women described in this book, only *The Rule*. I will describe the many and not the few. I am no dummy, I already know the first thing to discredit this book is to say, "Well, I know chicks that aren't like this," or for women who decide to take a personal investment while reading to say,

"I know he's not talking about me because I would never be like that". I understand every single female in the world does not make the same choices and decisions and does not make the same mistakes. Only a fool would truly believe that. But let's be frank here, if women were the best decision makers, Maury or Jerry Springer wouldn't have a show. Am I right?

With all that being said, this is an account of just one man's thoughts and theories based off of his personal life experiences in his short time on this planet and hopefully, in return, there could be a few men out there that can vouch that also there was confusion and lack of understanding during their own endeavors dealing with women sometime in their lives. That way I'll know I wasn't crazy, just a man dealing with women in today's crazy world. I mean just check my credentials and let them be the measuring stick for my knowledge on this widely discussed topic. I was a navy brat, my dad served over twenty years, so we moved around a few places. But when I was almost ten, we settled in a little city in Louisiana. I'm talking Small Town, USA. So, you could imagine the quantity of females just running around that little hole in the wall box. Also, add on the fact that my parents were black Barbie and Ken. The Colgate smiles having, front cover of *Perfect Looking Couples* magazine type of beautiful relationship I was privileged to absorb on a daily basis my entire childhood. Pops, the honorable, intelligent, hardworking, handsome, respectable husband and father. Mom, the beautiful, smart, driven, best cook and most loving lady in my life. And her resumé, don't even get me started. She married my dad in her late teens, one love, one real relationship, and only one person she's ever been with in her entire life.

I know that sounds foreign. Who in the world saves themselves for one man in their life anymore? I'm familiar with that saying: "You have to kiss a lot of frogs to find your prince" but in my situation, this upbringing would be the example that would forever define the way I view women and the shaping of relationships moving forward. My parents used to always give me little sayings like, "If a girl is with you and loves you and you know she loves you and tells you no, then you know she's not telling anyone else yes." And, "if she's sleeping around, don't be around." I mean I lived my entire teenage to young adult life based off things my parents told me. Their relationship advice was the Bible to me. Why not take what was told by them so seriously, I ask. They were married, didn't abuse or cuss each other and seemed genuinely happy together. I believed the only way that I was to continue tradition and follow suit was to look for someone that reminded me of my amazing mother. That was the only real way that I felt at the time to feel special to someone. Being the first love, the first everything. Knowing I'm the first, who could she compare me to?

I'm the first guy to make her feel something she's never felt before, so that has to be absolute truth, right? That became the starting point and ultimate blueprint to how I was going to find my future wife. Man, what an adventure and unforeseen reality check that transformed my perception on everything I was taught at a young age. The views that I learned and inherited during my "love journey" truly gave me the insight and knowledge to bring this book to this moment. There were just entirely too many stories and experiences that I would jot down from time to time to not want to share with the fellas. So, this is my written growth and realization. Figuring out that just because it was, does not mean that it still is. And once you finish all of the pages and make it to the end of this experience, then you'll truly understand what that means. Enjoy.

II.

#SituationshipGoals

It was a hot summer day. Now, I'm from the south so hot summer days are all relative. Hot is hot. But this day was particularly hot for some reason. Why I chose to run through the park with my headphones bumping Black Eye Peas "Let's Get It Started" that day, I guess I'll never really know. You don't understand, it was easily two hundred and eleven degrees with absolutely no wind and no I don't do drugs. So, about twenty minutes into the run is when I jog across this, a couple on a bench under a gazebo in the shade arguing. Now, I see couples arguing all the time. It's a common form of communication in relationships. As I think about it, the times that I encounter people together that choose not to argue, I either assume they just finished arguing or have been letting the confrontation simmer for a while and later on that day at their home, it's going to be war. This particular argument, however, with the gazebo couple intrigued me more from the physical aspect than the verbal ping pong assaulting. This couple looked straight out of a comic book. The girl was a beautiful, tall, blonde bombshell. She could have played a lifeguard on the show *Baywatch,* nothing short of a Victoria's Secret angel. The guy on the other hand was this big, fat, sloppy ZZ Top beard having, messy looking kind of man. I try not to judge. I can't stress that enough. I continue to work on universal unconditional acceptance every day. Nobody is perfect and I, for one, am as far from perfection as one can get. But in this scene, it wasn't just the look of the couple arguing that garnered my undivided attention. It was how the man completely dominated and overthrew the argument from start to finish. He was laying into this beauty queen with insults and demeaning language with no remorse at all. His female companion on the other hand, stood there and took the verbal jabs and uppercuts with the chin of an undefeated heavyweight world champion. It appears he wasn't even attacking her with harsh and violent rhetoric at all. Just a glazed over blank look as if the man screaming at her was a simple piece of glass art. From the time I noticed this couples one-sided disagreement to the time I was passing by, it looked as though the rumbling had subsided and assumed to have hit its dramatic conclusion. Right at my moment of totality, however, I saw the bearded pirate swiftly reach out and grab his lady's arm and begin to drag her off. That moment my spidey senses morphed, and I began my plan of action called, "Operation- Don't Let the Blonde Chick Die." Note that most of the time I tend to mind my own business. My first instinct, finish my run and go home. But at that time all I could see was the news headlines in my mind, "White Woman Gets Attacked, Black Guy Jogs By". And I knew I wouldn't be able to sleep with that event burned into my good conscience. Maybe I'm paranoid or something, but I just normally don't take chances like that. Maybe it was the extreme heat that day that completely fried the part of my brain that makes sensible, intelligent decisions, who knows? But what I saw next made me stop my notion to drop down and do push-ups to prepare for battle with this sea monster of a man. The same time this man was dragging his trophy girl off with one hand, he was reaching in his pocket with his free hand and pulled out keys and hit the buttons to light up a brand-new Colgate white, fully loaded, big, bodied Mercedes G wagon. I stopped dead in my tracks to process the scene thoroughly.

Of course, that's why that lady could absorb so much verbal karate from that man with a Coca-Cola smile on her face. She's not invested in this guy; she's invested through this guy. I used to believe women were all just as tough as my mom is. A no-nonsense, "Who do you think you're talking to?", "If you don't respect me, there's no need for us to talk" type. Also, all I ever heard on the radio and saw on TV growing up were these tough independent female groups singing all these women empowering anthems that females sang loud in their cars and screamed to the top of their lungs in the clubs and concerts. Groups like Destiny's Child, En Vogue, TLC, and the list goes on and on. Showing young ladies all over that submission is a crime and promoting the phrase that is preached to this day that "I can do bad all by myself". The mind-blowing issue that has rarely been addressed or even discussed is how what is portrayed on different media and social outlets and what is actually seen and practiced in actual accounts is on completely opposite spectrums of reality.

The truth is women can tolerate a lot. I mean we don't give women enough credit for how much they can **choose** to put up with. A woman's breaking point is really determined by how much concrete she has supporting her foundation. The more a woman has to support her, the longer it will last and less likely her fall will take place. Let's say a female is supported financially by a man and when I say financially supported, I mean her basic needs and even extravagant wants are all met by the swipe of this man's credit card. **Women in these positions aren't loyal to the man, they're loyal to the situation.** If the situation benefits the woman, she stays involved with the man. If it does not or no longer does, she will lose interest and effort towards that situation and look elsewhere. But they are not in a committed relationship. It's not about commitment, it's about comfort.

Now, I know you might be saying to yourself, ok, good for her. She's using him for money but can still go off and find a man that she really wants to be with besides just for the money and be with him. To that I say, I agree with you wholeheartedly. Now consider the consequences. The guy that's acting as a corporate sponsor for this particular female's "business expenses" treats this circumstance as a contractual obligation for the woman to remain sexually consistent and committed to him and only him. If she breaks those simple rules, it would be considered a breach of contract and his financial obligations are abruptly and immediately terminated, even though the man and woman may or may not have any real feelings towards each other. They may or may not even want to be together but because both parties benefit from the other doings, they act, live, behave, and correspond with the outside world as a legit couple. That is what's called a **SITUATIONSHIP.** A situationship can be an enhancement and also a detriment to a person's life and well-being. I showed you one example of a benefit with that being a sexual and financial advantage. The hardship behind a situationship is simply time. The longer a woman stays in a situation, the more comfortable she becomes. This creates contentment and that prohibits the woman from thinking clearly enough towards the want to pursue a true meaningful relationship with someone who enhances her life rather than just her bank account. It also complicates it if a child becomes involved. It's very unfortunate when a baby is born in an environment with two parents with no true bond or even want for one. The clock after a circumstance life is now revved up super-fast in the direction of ending the situationship instead of adding time to it. The man now feeds two people and if and when the woman's body changes, does the attraction now change, since beauty and body was the main course for the situationship in the first place. That's just one example and an opinionated possibility anyway.

I can remember my friend was really excited about this one girl he started courting one day. And what I mean by courting was this woman taking him out and buying him things. Just his presence was the only thing required by the woman. In less than a month, he moved in and became a permanent house sitter for his new "girlfriend". She fed him, clothed him, and let him use her car. She pretty much was the Yvette to his Jodi. Yes, Baby Boy'd him. A woman would only be acceptable towards this type of situationship due to the control and accessibility it provided. She supports the man in hopes of him being in a comfortable enough state to less likely to sway towards another woman and leave her entirely. Plus, with the guy not being in a position to support himself, it's easier to keep a GPS like track on his daily mobility. His places to roam become limited and transportation becomes a daily negotiation. Given, a creative man can still figure out places to maneuver and if he still cheats and entertains another woman, he can still very well do so. All I'm saying is this specific situationship puts the woman in a position of power and gives her the majority leverage. There are productive situationships and less positive ones. Sometimes situationships can turn into actual relationships. Other times, it's just a massive ticking timebomb waiting to detonate once set off, Can leave nothing but hurt feelings and more emotional issues added to reasoning to why women and men have resistance to trust and commitment. That's why knowing the difference between true relationships and the alternative is so key. Also, the **monkey bar** method tends to dilute real long-term love and staying power due to its effectiveness and cultural acceptance. Even though situationships should be an understood agreement, the fear of loss and uncompensated time plus, significant damage to ego sometimes is the reason enough for many women to shy away from them only after experiencing and losing from one. Yes, women want things, a want for financial security. **Women love what a man does _for_ them. Men love what a woman does _to_ them.** Women go for who they want. They stay with what they think they deserve. But overall, women long for longevity. To know that the amount of time they invest into someone with payoff in the form of commitment long after their beauty and sex appeal that can obtain a situationship fades and a comfortable and rock steady circumstance remains.

<u>Need vs. Want</u>

There's a great book I had the pleasure of reading called *The Reckoning* by Philip Finch. A great novel about life and love. Not to give away the entire story for those few people who have not read it yet, it just gave a great example of need versus want. To paraphrase, it's the story of two brothers, Billy and Matty, who both care for the same girl they grew up with named Kate. She decided to be with Billy because he displayed what she felt she needed in a man and relationship. In a way, she settled to accept that Billy's love for her gets no better than what she felt she could get. But as soon as Matty shows interest, Kate instantly goes to Matty because he is what she genuinely wanted the entire time. **When the want is greater than the need, the want becomes the need.** Do women go as far as marriage to someone they settle for because marriage is the end goal for them? Or, having the best you can get is far more attractive than loneliness and marriage is just a secure participation trophy? Only the women involved can truly answer.

III.

Pretty Girls Don't Answer the Phone After 3AM

Everybody needs a job. Jobs help pass the time and create discipline to deter unproductive distractions. You could have called me Mr. Jobs. I've had over twenty in my life. That's correct. Those nine to five, W-2 tax collecting, can't wait for April but then have to owe jobs. Ever since I was nineteen, I averaged about two to three jobs a year. I'm in my thirties now so you can do that math. I enjoyed the night jobs the best. Not necessarily the graveyard shift jobs, those were some tough ones, especially the last few hours of the shift. By the time I got off work, it was around six or seven in the morning. All I had time for after that was to go to McDonald's, grab a McGriddle and orange juice, and finish that on the way home. Once I was there, shower, went to bed, and then woke up five hours later just to get ready and go to the other job. Remember I had a handful of jobs my life revolved around. This one particular job I remember working was fun. I used to deliver pizza at night. Twenty deliveries a shift was the goal because then I made over one hundred in tips and that was a good night for me.

Hold up, let me get back on track. I just kind of miss those simpler days. But once I got off work on Fridays, there was this bar I would go to. It was a nice little spot that would be packed on the weekends. So, this one particular Friday I'm in this bar, minding my own business working on my dance moves. When this heaven-sent masterpiece of a lady walks in. The type of women that I know God put in front of Adam to test him to eat that apple. She had that big curly long hair that I'm weak for, light eyes, full lips, and thighs that were screaming to bust out of those jeans. Not to forget, she had so much booty it could be seen from the parking lot. Now most of the time for me at least, these are the types of women I would admire, wave at, view the large ring on their finger, and then imagine how happy their husbands are. Call it luck, divine promise, whatever. But this woman had no ring and no accomplice. I either make my move now or spend the rest of my life yelling at my future wife about what I could have had.

So, I did. I walked right up to her, smiled, did a Bobby Brown spin, and smoothly reached my hand out. She busted out laughing and hugged me. Touchdown. Hey, I'm the man when I want to be. Trust me, I'm no slouch. But to make a long story short, we had a great night talking, laughing, and dancing as I observed the jealous looks of every guy in the bar with my side eye. We even ate at the Waffle House after the bar shut down. Perfect start to a beautiful relationship, right? We exchange numbers, part ways, and on the way, she calls me just to tell me she had the best time with me and can't wait to see me again. Checkmate. Time to change my relationship status on Facebook. I mean she's the girl I've been waiting and longing for. My time has come.

The next morning, I text her good morning with the smiley face emoji, wake up, and get ready to start my adventure with my new lady. Two hours later, no response. No big deal, it's only noon. She easily could have slept in late. I start my day. Fast forward to four o'clock. Still no text. So, I gave her a call. Phone rings to her voicemail. No need to leave a message. So, I shake it off and go to the gym after work. Now I'm back home and it's after six. No text, no call. Eight shows up and my phone lights up. A text comes in and my day making, "hey wya?" message is what I'm ready to read as I open my phone. But instead, the dreaded "hey, who's this?" instead shows itself. Now, how in the world can a girl that just told me less than twenty-four hours ago that she had the best time and can't wait to see me again tomorrow, text me a confusing "who's this?" So not only did she not acknowledge us seeing each other today like we planned, but didn't even have the common courtesy to save my number? Or so I thought. How could this be? Where did it all go so horribly wrong?

Then it dawned on me. It's not that she forgot about the exciting time she had with me the previous night. Or that she even forgot to save my number. This young lady's calendar is full of great times and opportunities to not have to save any numbers. What does she lose if the same experience can be relived the next night? See, extremely attractive single women live in a type of déjà vu vortex, where a woman can go through a cycle of favorable opportunities and experiences regularly. I'm talking limitless desirable moments. Now, there was a time where opportunity was only presented through a face-to-face encounter. So, a woman only had as many opportunities as her physical in person availability presented. But oh look how technology continues to be the game changer. Now due to social media and other advertising websites, a woman's chance of meeting men and winning opportunities to receive a plethora of best night evers has become infinite. What does a female truly lose by not saving a number or excusing herself from a date with a guy, if one second online or one click of the text message icon and her evening becomes a supermarket sweep of dinner and movie dates, cash and material gifts, cars, modeling jobs, homes, paid bills, and whatever a man can provide with a swipe or withdrawal? Tarnishing the notion that one man at a time is the goal because multiple men is a reputation killer and bad for business. Today's market is quite common with women who may carry with them more than one phone. She may walk with one phone for guys that she may like on a personal level and then another phone for the gentleman she may label as the ones she seeks a more business relationship with. The first rule of business, always give a get. It enables the chance for a female to acquire her wants and needs at a much faster pace. But diminishes the range of time a man has to sway these women in his direction to play for keeps. Sort of like speed dating with the turning knob on fastest. That's mostly in part of not just the quantity of men at a beautiful lady's disposal but also how she may view what quality men are all together. Let me put it in these terms. Let's say a young girl reaches the rightful legal age of eighteen. Now she has the approval to date any man she pleases. Well, what are the type of men to approach her first? The ones around college age perhaps. Or what about established young men in their mid to late twenties? Possibly business owners and corporate types in the thirty to forty range? Millionaire playboys in their fifties maybe? The point is **all types of men become possibilities.** Any and every man can flex their good looks or pocketbooks on an impressionable young woman as soon as she walks across the stage with her diploma in hand. It then becomes fair game. All that early influence can have a lasting effect on what a woman can prioritize most important in her lifelong term from what may seem the most important at that time in her life. **The great equalizer for women is <u>beauty</u>. The great equalizer for men is <u>money</u>.** Regardless of the consequence or circumstance, they are the factors that keep the person(s) in the game of love and partnership. Her opportunities only enhance and multiply as she matures and develops physically and mentally. So, for the remainder of a woman's best years or her "window," she hears every proposal, gimmick, deal, option, and come up you can imagine until she one, permanently chooses the suitor of her choice and becomes a family woman. Or two, her window expires and the carriage becomes a pumpkin where her opportunities dwindle, forcing her to make decisions based on needs and no longer just wants.

<u>A Woman's "Big Board"</u>

Women have a list numbered one through whatever towards how and what person they want to be with. Like in a draft, as the top prospects are drafted and then taken off the board or market, the best available then become the desired one once it's time to decide to choose a mate.

An older woman told me one time, "Women marry the richest guy that they can get, and men marry the most beautiful woman they can afford." I'm not too sure how accurate that statement truly is but from watching TV and looking at Instagram and TikTok that thought doesn't seem too farfetched.

<u>Choosing a man</u>

There's a game in these endangered buildings and rooms that are arcades that's called the claw machine. It's still in some restaurants, now that I think of it. I've seen one in a Golden Corral. But it's where you have a wide variety of prizes you can choose from. Stuffed animals, sports balls, candy, electronics, and all other types of miscellaneous items. The object is to take the claw and direct it to the gift that you want and drop the claw down to that gift, grab it, and then direct that prize to the hole where you can let the gift go and then reach down and receive it. The process that a woman goes through in choosing a man is very similar. The most appealing item in the cage is typically what is sought after first. The bad guy, the rich guy, the hard-to-get guy, the "his sex is the best in the world" guy. To where, every other guy that's in the pool of men start to become a distraction or barrier, putting themselves in the way of women's pursuit of their prize-winning, especially once that claw is dropped and the item is in a woman's possession. It now becomes an objective to take that giant stuffed teddy bear home or bust. As long as it looks as though forward momentum is taking place, the man, a.k.a. the stuffed bear, dropping out of the claw before reaching the dispense hole, is just a minor pause in the pursuit of receiving the gift; because as long as each drop is closer to the end, where the last drop was, it is no bother to the woman. In her eyes, she sees progression and soon possession of her prize.

The frustration doesn't come in the drops, it comes in stoppage of mobility. There comes a point where the teddy bear hits the glass wall and after that the claw, time after time, quarter after quarter, continues to drop the toy in the same spot that it dropped the last fourteen other times. Developing doubt and frustration to a woman because after all this forward movement and visons of a soon to be dream life with her man. Now, it turned to a stagnant game of wits and wasted time. Fourteen times turn into twenty times, and then into forty times. Now financially stressed and mentally drained, other toys in the prize pool go from distractions and barriers to viable options and opportunities for closure. The more frustrated the female, the more she just wants the process to be over. Women will push and pull at the man they want as long as he keeps moving toward what she wants. A relationship or some type of stable long-term commitment that could lead to marriage or if nothing else, locked in security. But once her guy no longer moves forward and especially tends to regress, a woman's eject button behind the break glass in case of an emergency catches her eye. Once that happens, she begins to look for her prize elsewhere. Instead of the giant stuffed animal, she moves to the plastic watch or the candy necklace. No, it's not what she initially wanted, but her main objective when she first touched the claw wasn't simply to get the bear. Even though yes, she may have spotted that first. But wanting a gift entirely because what a woman wants, is one thing, but if that fails, what she wants the most makes a suitable consolation prize. The good guy, the nine-to-five guy, the available guy, and "the best sex to me right now" guy. Having will always tend to outweigh not having and that can't be any more apparent than going after someone and it not working out versus going after someone and it does work. Which they may be able to obtain after just one or two tries.

IV.

The Daisy Effect

One of my favorite movies of all time to watch is *The Curious Case of Benjamin Button* for a few decisive reasons. One of them being the movie was based and shot in New Orleans, one of my favorite places to be and the other for the lifelong relationship between the star characters Benjamin and his love interest Daisy. Her story was a remarkably familiar Hollywood one, duplicated in multiple movies including the female co-star Jenny in the classic movie *Forrest Gump*. Daisy's life was not as graphic and chaotic as Jenny's was but was just as impactful and sad all the same. Jenny was molested as a young girl and that horrific experience dictated her decision making for the rest of her life. One troubled relationship after another, battles with drug addiction with little to no remorse for her destructive lifestyle until the very end. All the while, her "knight in shining armor," Forrest Gump, was convinced to wait for his loves' "finding herself" period of her life, until she was ready for a relationship, after every poor choice there was to make, that ultimately dictated her eventual demise. That was Jenny's story.

Daisy's was a tad bit more understandable and relatable to the type of women I've had the pleasure of being in the presence of. It was a fascinating encounter between the two main characters. Daisy and Benjamin, without giving the movie away, (which you should have already seen anyway, it's over ten years old, plus it's a classic) met young and Benjamin knew from the beginning that Daisy was the one true special person he met and wanted in his life. But like most movie love stories I've seen, the two initially could not be. Benjamin went his own way and Daisy went into the transformation from young woman to actual adult woman through the fast phase, where a young lady embarks on a slew of sexual experiences perceiving them as steps towards adult womanhood. Now, the situations and experiences may change female to female but the influence and change to mindset is all identical. See Daisy went through life away from Benjamin, believing that big city life and free love with drinking and other nightlife endeavors all played intricate parts towards blossoming into a woman. Just like women in the real world, it's no different. Young women use sex as an opportunity to rebel against the contrary to what was told to them at an early age. That idea that that sex is a grown-up thing and should only be participated by adults. Therefore, if she is to be an adult, sex must play a part.

Now, as a biased man with no daughters, I would not have no issue with that mentality. Just imagine a world where sex flowed into men's life like water or consistent hit on the slot machines in the casino. Yes, STDs and other sexual infections would run rampant and ultimately destroy the world. With all that being said, the free sex is still a nice thought. All if it wasn't for one small unequivocal reason to why open sexual lifestyles for women are so detrimental to their future well being. Just one word, emotion. The fact that once a female has sex with someone to where an emotional attachment forms, it no longer becomes just another experience to validate womanhood. The female, especially if she's invested in the guy she's sexual with, now pursues in the direction that her emotions are leading her. Look at a woman's emotions as a game of tug of war. On one team, you have the woman's mind and on the other team, her heart. Nine times out of ten, the heart pulls the mind across the line, winning the match. Now, the lady is consumed with the notion of having more than just sex with the man and if the man experiences the exact tug of war moving his heart in the exact same direction, a happy conclusion ensues.

Now, please allow me to play devil's advocate towards this thought. Let's just assume that this particular sexual encounter doesn't lead into anything more than what it was originally set as. Sex. So, everybody wins, right? The woman gains her sexual experience towards womanhood and the man just benefits from being at the right place at the right time. Hold up, wait a minute. Not only does that not become a sexual experience toward womanhood, but now becomes a tally towards times a female had sex with a male and nothing else transpired from it. Perception plays the drums. Remember when you were in elementary school, and you had a behavior chart? I had a behavior chart based on the letters A through F. A meaning you had exceptional behavior. A tremendous joy to be around. F meant you were a menace. The teachers most hated students. And B through D was everywhere in-between. Look at every relationship, attempt at a relationship, even a situation that seemed like a relationship that all failed as a clothes pin moved from the A board to the B and so on and on. Before long, the woman has a negative look at sex and what it could mean after the actions take place. Emotional walls tend to go up, forcing a man to endure another obstacle towards winning a woman's heart. Negative attitudes towards relationships became an act one, transferring fear of a great relationship with someone due to the multiple bad endings of her past and lack of experiencing happy ones. Some women take many unfortunate experiences to turn their mind away from positive thoughts toward sex. Others only need one. Simply because **women give sex for love, men give love for sex**. Women tend to believe that sex it a gift given and not a just a reward for themselves. Once the sex is given and there's no love, only disappointment pursues.

I know women say they think about sex as much as men and that's a fair assessment. I've met a few women in my life who no matter what the outcome, if the sex was exceptional, satisfaction was guaranteed. But I'm not referring to those women. After you've had everything except the sex you wanted, why not pursue just that? Let's say a woman just wants sex, nothing else. And after the experience is over, the guy gets dressed, leaves, and goes home. The next day, no text messages, no social media conversation, and no phone call. If the woman is content with just the sex, then no hard feelings, right? My point is that, if there was another way women could gain a lifelong relationship without having sex to receive it, how many women today would sign up for that option? It's also another way to create change.

Something traumatic or dramatic also can happen to redirect a woman's mindset towards sex, love, relationships, and everything related. Again, not to ruin great movies but like I've said before, you should have seen those classics by now. In *Forrest Gump*, Jenny's life is destructive and completely reckless. Then, she receives news that adjusts her life in a direction that becomes more appealing and beneficial towards Forrest's favor. In *The Curious Case of Benjamin Button*, it was less than the actual life spinning out of control, but more of one isolated incident that occurred in Daisy's life that forced change in her life. But on a more relatable thought directed towards women, it was her understanding that her getting older is making her see the way she's living life as something that change is not just wanted, but necessary.

Overall, the lesson I saw that was learned, was that two major moments in a woman's life will swing the pendulum in the direction of change. One way, is simply a repeated action with the same consequences not in her favor. Then age will finally sway her towards a new view of her pursuit of a happy long-term relationship. The second is a traumatic, unanticipated event in a woman's life that forces legitimate change in her life. Whether that change is unintentional or sometimes intentional. Motherhood, a sexually transmitted disease, or even a physical injury. An event that lessons her options of men and prevents her to simply rely on looks to advance her personal goals and ambitions with the opposite sex. Either way, eventually a female will figure out life out and eradicate the error of her ways. When she decides to do so is simply a sky dive, she'll choose to participate in once she's ready to jump.

V.

If Self-Esteem Came in a Can

Me and my friend were close, really close. I call him my homeboy. He has some of the greatest qualities you can possess in being a first class go getter. He works three jobs every single day. He is a mechanic in the early morning, works at a warehouse during the day, and then a restaurant at night. He really makes more than enough money just being a cook at that fancy restaurant. He even auditioned for *Top chef* and almost made it to the contestants that make it on the show. I had to ask him one day.

I said, "Man, what's your problem? You don't have any kids. The bills are paid. You have a nice house. Vacation time pretty much whenever you want. Yet, you still manage to invest all your time and life into spending your twenty-four hours working. Therefore, cutting into our party time. Why?"

His dumb response was the reason we were so close.

He simply said, "I got to work. It's just me. I don't know and don't care to know anything else. I am who I am."

Now I'm usually compassionate and just too lazy when it comes to analyzing people's justifications for why they do what they do. My general response was normally conditioned with an understanding head nod and high-five. But not in this particular occasion. I was determined to get to the bottom of my friend's response and find a reasonable solution to his passive nature. The more I thought about it, the more I pieced the puzzle together. My homeboy is the ultimate hustler, not just due to his love for money and purpose. He has an incredible fear of loss. He doesn't gamble because he tells me he hates losing money. No scratch-off tickets, lottery picks, dice games, not even automatic week one college football picks, knowing that over ninety percent of major power five teams are playing cupcake schedules. Nothing. After many long, extensive conversations with his father, I came to discover that when my friend was younger, he lost everything to a major flood. His shoes, clothes, electronics, you name it. So, after that experience, he dedicated himself to obtaining a financial safety net to protect his future possessions and well-being from a previous unfortunate fate. It was his past that shaped his present, many ways in a positive direction, by molding his self-drive and hunger for hard work and success. But also, that mindset created some setbacks, keeping him from experiencing what the world offers due to some risk being required to obtain them. He won't even ride a jet ski, not because of the sharks or dangerous fish, but the rental time ending before he gets the full amount of ride time he paid for. I know it's ridiculous, but he can't help it. It's embedded in him.

It's a common balance that shaped our lives due to the experiences we have had or haven't had yet. Some things happened to us, so we become this. Things happen, so we became that. What if it wasn't just what a person went through, but what they saw that shaped their life decisions? When you really look at it, optics influence as much internal as external.

For example, I knew a woman who had a three-year-old son. She raised him by herself and worked long hours at her job. So, she asked me one day if I could drop her little man off at daycare. I had no issue with that, so I told her no problem. Now, before I get into my point of influence, allow me to set the point up with the description of my friend's son. This kid looked like a movie star. He had a head full of wavy, curly hair, light brown eyes and the million-dollar smile already mastered. I knew he was going to be a little heartbreaker in no time. So, I drove him to the day care, walked him inside into the playroom where all the other little kids were playing, and like magnets to a refrigerator door, all these little girls started charging at my friends' son. I felt like I was security at a Chris Brown concert. Just about every girl at that daycare came running. Even the ones that weren't interested in talking to the little boy just ran over simply to see what the fuss was all about.

Right there in that innocent beautiful moment, my never-ending thoughtful mind started wondering and analyzing. I saw the pretty girls, the not so pretty girls, the chubby girls, the girls with the Coke bottle glasses, and one girl I'm quite sure was a boy all rushing to the front with reckless abandon. No pause to sit back for a second to think, "Maybe there's too many girls all at once sweating this boy, I'll just back off. Or do I even have a chance with this kid? What if he's full of himself and just uses me and then leaves me for a 'better girl'?" Or even the thought, "If I talk to him, will he hurt me like the last boy I was with?" Where were all these concerns and reservations? Where had the hesitation towards the pursuit gone?

Ok, yes, I realized those were little girls who had no business asking or even thinking those type of questions. Knowing anything dealing with relationships or how they should be feeling about themselves. But that's my point. Where and when is the turning point in a young girl's life when she goes from confident, reckless little boy chaser, to reserved, cautious, hurt, "I'll never love again" grown woman? In order to find the solution, you have to discover the source of the problem. There was this long snake shaped device that you hooked up to a box to transmit power. It was used to show these multiple flashing images called cable network channels, where families used to gather around and watch great non-reality show programming. Relaying wonderful messages and lessons we all could relate to and grow from. Ah, yes. The TV a.k.a. the self-confidence killer.

I have a little sister. Well, she's not little anymore. She's a grown woman who has her own life and is a mother. So, I'll just say I had a little sister. A little sister who cared about two things, chips and Disney movies. Not dresses, not adding more volume to her hair, and definitely not impressing any boys. None of the girls around the neighborhood at the time cared about any of that. Then like sand through the hourglass, so came change. It went from girls around my corner stopping the ice cream man every day at five PM to diet drinks and low-calorie cookies. It just didn't make any sense. These girls weren't fat at all, so why the extreme dietary lifestyle at such an early age? Simple, one hair commercial on TV with a response from my little sister saying, "She's so pretty; look at her," and enough light bulbs go off in my head to accommodate prom.

See, it's not just what females see that makes them want to look that way. My sister saw pretty girls at school and at home, no big deal. But the ones on TV were different. They were beautiful and on TV. So that meant they were a success. That's the measuring stick. Beauty with bright lights. From teen movies, where the beautiful sexy cheerleader gets the strapping handsome star quarterback, to the slim, fit blonde bombshell that wins that beauty pageant, TV images kick the confidence right out of young women on a regular basis. Engraving the notion that if you look like this, that life also comes with it. Not even just TV. Real life has the same negative impacts from time to time. Not only is attractive imagery on the agenda for young females, but also the company of a young gentleman is a red-hot item on the to do list as well. See having a boyfriend or man, boo, bae, husband, or whatever titles women are in pursuit of, it's like the matching hat with the matching shoes. She goes with one.

Now back to the TV example. Find me one network that doesn't have at least one TV show or a movie where the man caresses the woman and gazes into her eyes to tell her he loves her with every breath in his body. Then, whisks her off in his arms as they somehow glide up on a romantic sailboat and then ride on into the moonlight glistened water, destined for happiness and eternity. See that's the draw. Not the romantic man or the loving words he speaks, but the end game. *The Crazy Rich Asians* movie marriage, the house with the kids running around ready for lunch and the matching tattoos and jumpsuits for Valentine's Day. If women could just do all those things by themselves, they wouldn't need men. You can call us men a glorified DJ at an album release party. Yes, the party can still be done without us, but somebody has to spin the records, right?

So, we've established that A. Females are attracted to imagery portrayed on TV and real life. And B. Men make great accessories. Understanding that moves dissect how women go about obtaining these goals in life. The first part is simple. You choose to look a certain way, take those steps to obtain that look. Stereotypical beauty consists of makeup. Better body? Proper diet and exercise. Seems simple enough. The other part presents the greatest challenge. The "getting the man" part. See women do an extraordinary job of asking questions. If I received a dollar every time a female interested in me interrogated me with a barrage of questioning, I'd have so much money, I would have never got around to write this book. Yes, women are world champion question askers. They do so to process and compare answers. What they might have already heard and what can be stored in the memory bank. But when it comes to asking the right questions, that's where the issues lie. Women tend to only ask the type of questions they either already know the answers to or questions that the safest answers come attached. The answers women don't want to know lie in the questions they don't ask. Ladies rarely ask what men want. They just assume. Maybe read up on those magazines with the hilarious articles titled "Ways to Please your Man." I laugh every time I come across those stories. Instead of women just simply asking men what we want, they tend to just adapt the microwave approach because it's quick and accommodating.

I had a conversation with a group of women at a bar one time after work. You know me, always doing some research.

I just simply asked them, "What do you ladies think men want?"

The responses I received prompted me to add more chapters to this book. The answers I got from these women were about as generic as a box of great value cupcakes. One woman told me sex, another said hoes, one said a weak woman, another gave me "a lot of strippers". She was nice. I came to find out these women were single as a dollar bill and just chose that night to vent their frustrations to me because their love lives have been karate kicked all over the place and resentment and grudge remained. Did they blame the men for their relationship mishaps? Absolutely. You don't need me to tell you that women rarely if ever take responsibility for failed relationships. If you had been in one with a woman, then you already knew that.

The three things numbered shape a woman's life
1.   What she went through
2.   When she went through it
3.   Who was around at the time it happened

What I'm saying is simply, why are women saying that? Why was sex the very first thing brought up when I asked the group what do men want? It's the easiest approach. Like I said before, women give men little to no credit towards knowing desires and requirements from the fairer sex. But accept misguided expertise. **Women want family, commitment, and security. Men want loyalty, support and trust.** It all falls back on a battered self-confidence. If women believed that if they just told jokes and were funny a man would fall in love with them, would dates be more entertaining? If a woman approached a man by showing and proving to him that no matter the circumstance her support and loyalty wouldn't faulter keeping him by her side, would wedding and engagement ring purchases be at an all-time high? I can't answer that but, what I can say is that sex is the easiest approach and women believe that's the largest draw for men, anyway. All while completely disregarding the many other talents and blessings that women may possess just as much influence. Just go for the bunt. Shoot the high percentage shot. Run for it on third and one. In theory, it really does make sense. If sex is really and truly what men want the most, why wouldn't you present that first? Unless that act benefits from a high success rate, which it does not. But what else would you lead with if you had little to no confidence in anything else provided in your nonexistent arsenal? Everything mentioned always reverts back to self-esteem and confidence. The higher a woman's confidence, the more powerful and uplifting her traits are coming at you with no kickback from failed attempts from the past. Because let's be honest, who talks about the losses when all you want is the win? The proof is in the pudding, but the recipe is the issue. As a young woman goes through her life, the purity and originality of herself is put to the test on a regular basis. It's up to her self-worth and abilities within herself to dodge and maneuver through life, missing the exits that stop progress and continue down the highway of separating herself from the pack to become the woman that you just don't find every day. Is life a treacherous and unforgiving road? Yes, there's no doubt about that. But that's why the term "wife material" isn't just thrown out like beads during a Mardi Gras parade. Also, making a man's life that much more satisfying once he finds her, not just from knowing what one looks like, but from knowing one who doesn't.

VI.

The Law of Balance

When I was younger, maybe right out of high school, I remember going over to my friend's place and would see his collection of black men's magazines out for me to view. Back then, in the good old days, there were magazines that showcased the curviest, most beautiful women of all colors, that myself and other like-minded men considered a must-have. I can recall my homeboy passing an issue to me and it was the Smooth magazine with the superstar model Esther Baxter on the cover.

See, back when there was a time where music companies spent millions of dollars on Rap videos, a selected group of physically gifted females were chosen specifically to enhance the quality of the visual experience. Women like Melyssa Ford, Vida Guerra and Esther Baxter just to name a few. I knew right then and there looking at all those magazines like King, Smooth and Show Girl, the physical type of female I wanted to spend the rest of my life with, that I truly believed at that time would bring me blissful happiness. See, I saw a woman visually and accepting that to the table as The beauty. Every man wants a woman that he is physically attracted to claim as his own. True. Although, that saying, "what glimmers isn't always gold" holds weight, simply because it's correct. Someone may look one way but the visual could be coating over something that isn't very shiny at all. The new saying should be: "a pretty face won't guarantee a pretty place," all due to the fact that for the most part you have to pick and choose jewelry now.

There was a store in the mall I used to go to, I'm not sure if that store is still around or not. A lot of time has passed since these moments, but the place was called Build-a-Bear, where you could go in and assemble whatever kind of bear your heart desired. A black bear with blue eyes and sneakers wearing a cop uniform. You could make that happen. Look at that scenario in the way of a female. Of course, in a perfect world we would all desire the lady with the pretty face, great body, who cooks, cleans, works, great attitude, loyal, ambitious and the perfect partner in crime. Now pinch yourself, you awake? Ok good, now let's continue.

A time before social media, before likes, before followers and direct messages, an attractive woman didn't really have a true understanding of her beauty. Unless she was discovered by an opportunist on the street, beauty had no instant market value. Yes, family members and strangers would declare admiration and attraction verbally, but women didn't wake up to a plethora of messages and comments regularly reflecting the same vibe. So all modern technology did was declare to a female that she was indeed the pretty person she always wanted to be. Therefore, attention is now drawn to that. More likes and more followers to feed that intense craving of acceptance. So if all the attention goes to the machine that is social media, then more opportunity follows. With more eyes on her, a woman can receive more outside offers from companies, men, even other women wanting to use that beauty for personal and corporate gain. So now a good-looking lady not only has multiple love interests at her disposal but also financial offers at every turn. So what space does that leave in her life for change of direction? Easy: not much.

Who has time for domestic capacity, culinary expertise or even steadfast loyalty through the good and bad rollercoaster of love? If things get bad and no longer compliments a lady's life goals, she can just simply delete your page and proceed to scroll to the next one. It's not easy to be in a position with women with so much leverage. Did not say impossible, just not easy.

There was a time when women possessed many different techniques at her disposal to pull the man she desired. If she was beautiful, she had that. If she could cook and clean, she had that. If she was business savvy and could help a man triple his money, that was her finger roll. Somehow from that time in space to present day, the playbook has adjusted. No longer are all things a possibility for each and every woman.

Have you ever noticed why you see certain women with multiple qualities and others without any? More specifically, the groups of women. I once knew a group of exceptionally beautiful women who used to attend this club every Friday like clockwork. Every last one of them had their hair right, nails done, and dressed to the nines. They looked like a gang of basketball wives. I always asked myself what men in their right minds would be attached to these dream girls and not be the happiest, most satisfied guys in the world? Just my luck, I happened to meet one of those insanely lucky gentlemen who dated one of the "blessed four" whom I titled them. One day I met up with him and simply asked him straight up what it was like to wake up every single day to a beauty queen sandwich? He actually laughed, and told me that his relationship isn't really what it seems to be.

He proceeded to completely disappoint me by describing his goddess was drama filled, not very sexual, disrespectful, and couldn't boil water. The allegations at that time were bothersome and saddening. I had to ask him how he was still with this girl if she wasn't making him feel like a million dollars on the regular. This guy had a good job, a nice place, a great car and didn't look like Flavor Flav. He looked straight in my face and re-arranged my life with the following words: His girl didn't do any of the things that he wanted because she didn't have to.

Men knew she didn't provide much else besides beauty and for the most part, they accepted that whole-heartedly. It's in part that women do what they have to in order to achieve what they want to. If they don't have to, they won't. So where does that leave for the ladies that aren't seen on the most wanted list for men, but still desire relationships, marriage and family? Well, that's easy. I call them the Intangibles. The abilities seen today as extra or plus traits that women possess, that were at one time seen as necessities to portray them as wife material.

I know a lady I'll call Katie. Katie was no movie star. Internalized no ability to shift a room simply with her presence. Average face and was shaped like a post office mailbox. What she lacked in physical stature, she overcame with overwhelmingly positive energy. She was kind, directing enchanting conversations effortlessly. A huge sports fan who knew the entire ninety-six Chicago Bulls roster, even the bench players. Could cook a mean steak, and didn't shy away from sex discussions. On paper she was a keeper, it just didn't materialize in person. She possessed the "But" factor. A woman's ability to recognize how to pivot from initial rejection while moving back towards the path to achieve her ultimate end goal. Some women can spin move a no just to get a first down yes. I don't have a big booty <u>BUT</u>. I'm not the prettiest girl <u>BUT</u>. Then, follow it up with a positive alternative attribute. That is all a mindset few women possess. Katie was a diamond in the rough.

Is it so easy to categorize women like that though? If you take a Katie and you glamorized her like you would a VH1 Love and Hip Hop Beauty. Same image and stature, would you have the same lady or a completely different person? What I've seen is the way that a woman carries herself or even how she even pursues her future is all based on the options and opportunities presented. You see professors and elected officials, engineers for NASA and check academic credentials and great resumes. Do you base that success off of pure drive and determination or simply due to little-to-no male distractions or early opportunities to pursue other careers in modeling, social media influencing or even early retirement from pursuing the sugar baby business? If every single woman was presented the same exact opportunities in the same consistent way to get whatever it is that women would want out of life, which ones would still pursue the tough road to success and who would take the road less challenging?

Mrs. Meatloaf*

Invites to dinner makes me nervous. Not so much the whole cliché "what to wear" mode, "what bottle of wine to grab," or "topics to discuss or dismiss" thought process but more of the type of food that will be served that creates the most uneasiness for me. I simply won't eat anyone's food. Period. Washed hands before and after prepping is a must have, and me not knowing that whole heartedly beyond a reasonable doubt is enough to just respectfully decline the meal entirely and enjoy a sensible egg and cheese sandwich from the safe, clean confines of my own dwelling.

This invite, however, was more of an unavoidable beg and tug from a coworker who I not only enjoyed working with, but actually enjoyed spending time with after the clock was punched. He asked me, well, more insisted, I come over for dinner with his wife who can prepare and I quote "food that will knock your draws off". With overwhelming confidence like that and trusting there's no e-coli involved. I reluctantly agreed.

So there I was that evening, ringing the doorbell to my coworker's home, my OCD pouring out of my feet and neck just waiting to see the end of this event, so I can hurry home and wash my hands and shower my skin off. Then soon as I consider skipping this evening of fear and regret, the door opens and standing in front of me, I was assuming the wife. Dressed in a blue summer dress that was designed to fit snug around her curves, but since her curves were more of a bow shape, her dress fit more like a toga. Equipped with a round chubby face, elf like ears, and this woman's appearance had me believe I stumbled upon the wrong house and soon faced a trespassing charge. Just as I fix my mouth to apologize for disrupting her evening and walking away, my coworker buddy runs up behind her with his hand up high gesturing a high five, shouting, "Hey man, come on in."

Please allow me to explain why seeing his wife for the first time shocked me so much to the point I was ready to end the evening right then and there at the door. First. I'd never seen my friend's wife prior to that day. No pictures, no videos, no nothing. Never asked for one. My coworker never showed me. We only hung out a couple times and I try not to get too personal with people I don't spend a tremendous amount of time with. Don't get me wrong, my buddy was fun to be around, but so was my PlayStation. Needless to say, this dinner was unbecoming of me, and his wife's appearance threw me off. Not saying she was hideous or anything, because she was not. She just looked regular. I just knew that all the women at my job and any other woman who hung around us at work were crazy about my coworker. They blew him kisses, gave him way too long hugs and one even tried to show him some nudes of herself. All to which my work buddy just simply turned around and walked the other way. I just assumed that with him blocking all this lady love he was bombarded with, his wife had to be a centerfold or pro cheerleader at least. She was neither. And that was the only topic of discussion I was interested in having with him that evening.

I was led to their living room and was set down to an arrangement of different beverages neatly organized in a tin bucket of ice setting on a side of a glass table overrun with different snacks. My coworker came and sat down next to me as his wife went back to the kitchen to finish cooking. That meant the coast was clear for me to unleash an aerial assault of questions regarding his wife. Including went from dating to where he was, right at this very moment. He simply smiled and honestly told me that he understood his wife was no model and even went to the extent of saying his wife teases herself more than he ever could. He then assured me that in a short while, all my questions would be answered all at once in great detail. I just stared at him as I helped myself with chips and peanut M&Ms to give my-self time to piece this situation together all while controlling my OCD emergency alarm system. I was that distracted.

Dinner was soon called, and I was seated down to a wonderfully organ-ized dinner table with flowers, candles, and an elegant crystal centerpiece. My coworker's wife then set a plate down in front of me filled to the edge with a serving of 5 cheese macaroni, freshly grown and steamed seasoned green beans, delicious looking sweet candied yams and two hearty slabs of meatloaf coated with a brown and red sauce with a glaze of white cheese. Finished with homemade rolls. I never seen anything like that.

The entire time I was eating, it never occurred to me if hands were washed to prepare that meal or not. I didn't care. It was that delicious. I just looked up after I cleaned my plate to look at my coworker's wife as a tear trickled down my face. She smiled and simply told me, "I know. Thank you."

After dinner was finished and the plates were cleared, my co-worker and I were left to our own devices, he began to tell me the story about him and his wonderful wife. He explained to me that his wife approached him at a Walmart, asked for his number, which he was reluctant at first but ul-timately gave her because he so impressed with her direct and confident approach towards him. She called him the next day and invited him to din-ner where she would cook for him. Never quick to turn down a meal, he told me he agreed to her offer, went over, ate, and got a back rub and some other rubs I will fail to disclose. And after a repeated consistent method, eight years and a marriage and a baby later here he was. He told me his wife knows what he wants, when he wants it and makes his home the clean-est, most comfortable environment in his life. He told me that he was ac-tually doing me a favor by hanging out with me, because he would much rather be at home. I understood and got up. Shook his hand thanked his wife for the incredible meal. Walked out, shook my head, got in the car, and drove me and my new outlook home for the night.

<u>Beauty is the bar</u>

The great equalizer, beauty is the measuring stick and then everything else is her life, characteristics, qualities raise or lower that bar.

        Example: -----10 Beauty (Pros)

                ------5 Beauty (Cons)

VII.

You Can't Cheat with Empty Balls

I mean from a scientific standpoint, no duh, right? This is clearly a no-brainer. Should be as easy a chapter as any to comprehend. Not so fast my friend (in my Lee Corso voice). This is just a popular term used by a chef I worked with and many men alike. I don't really mean it in the literal sense. Of course, it's a challenge to be completely spent with a woman you just had sex with just to turn right around to have sex with someone else. Especially when you're getting older, where all you want to do after having explosive, body-draining sex is a sandwich and a nap. But I say to the contrary, it is possible. You can cheat with empty balls. Please allow me to shed light and explain the true meaning and use for this chapter's eye-catching title.

I've had my share of romantic encounters involving very capable and engaging ladies, no doubt. But what I have come to realize in my life is yes, sex is a very pleasurable two-way experience when done right. Where during these intimate exchanges, it would appear to me and the wonderful ladies would always be on the same page to how we would both want to enjoy our lovely moments. But after the end of a few experiences, it would appear to be the end of one event to assume me into believing the beginning of a new. The environment would seem to change; energy influenced by an awkward pause of almost concentrated thought, as though the woman's mind would be running in overdrive. Then, followed by a sudden rise up from the bed and sonic stage left. Now mind you, these extreme encounters would not happen on a regular basis. Most of the time, the lady would roll over and go to sleep or would convey herself to the bathroom for a shower, then afterwards, we would order pizza and watch a movie. Those, unfortunately, were all ideal circumstances where it came across my simple man mind, that these women I was blessed being with were all happy and satisfied. I tend to be more observant to the less ideal experiences I just mentioned earlier. It was more difficult to piece together the reasoning for such a sudden change moment to moment.

Now, I'm not referring to one-night stands. Those uncomfortable pieces of time, served truly trivial effects on me. I understood love and marriage possessed a significantly low success rate, therefore in those cases, sex would tend to be the beginning and end. I'm regarding to the times where I was involved with females that I was actually considering being exclusive with. Then, before I could suggest them to leave a toothbrush, these women would perform a Houdini disappearing act like it was legal. Now, I understand what I said in another chapter, that women give sex for love and men give love for sex. Which is accurate. But what had me head scratching was how the sexual activity would cease but the text messages directed me to accusations involving time with other women became the topic of discussion. Not in the present tense, like they just knew I was involved with other females at that moment, but more so the guessing game assuming since I enjoy sex, then intimacy with other women is imminent. At first, my answers to redirect the court room interrogation energy would tend to be "Well hey, if you were just having sex with me, there would be no other girls." Which, that just pissed women off to the fourteenth power. So, with me being the overthinker that I tend to be, I had to do a discovery to find out how and why these emotions from the women I was engaging in sex seems much like a see saw. Constantly topping over unto one side, then the next second raising up and dropping to the other. What I've come to realize, that astonished me after thinking for some time, while also engaging in conversations with women who have behaved this way towards men.

While I was contemplating so much over sex, I realized, that actually had nothing to do with it. It wasn't about sex at all. **It's all about Time.** The time that a woman decides that she wants a man to be her boyfriend to the time she no longer does. All sex does is accelerate the process. While I was sitting there believing that a woman made up her mind to no longer want to deal with me because she believes that all I wanted her for was sex, which yes is always a possibility, but I digress. The scenario at hand is when that is no longer the case. I've had women who choose to no longer pursue a relationship with me before sex could even take place. What these women were waiting on was confirmation. That one particular answer to a question. The way you don't text her back. The way you don't look at her when she looks at you. Or just the way tonight you wanted to have sex. All ways to justify the choice to leave you alone or to unprioritize you, becomes necessary. Don't get me wrong, there can be some circumstances where a female can continue to have sex with a guy with no commitment, proclamation or even a slight commitment. That's normally because her relationship time frame has yet to expire with him. Due to a few variables of course. One, she could put all her eggs into that one particular basket. Two, the other options in her phone could either be unreliable or non-committal. And three, the lady could actually just be that sexually satisfied and comfortable with the way that she's feeling at the moment.

Look, some women just really enjoy having sex. Emphasis on some. That notion that women want sex as much or even more than men is debatable. I believe that due to western cultural standards putting a label on the amount of people we sleep with can deter females from actually going out and having as much sex as they would want to, or at the least be un-apologetic about it. Still, that shouldn't take away from the actual wanting of sex. But, if you're one of these super bowl champion men who walk around with the "drained grapes" due to your woman or women sexing you to pieces, good for you. If you're in a committed relationship with one of these blessed children of the great almighty, please remember, the best deals for engagement rings are during late fall and winter. Just don't let that woman go. Now, there is an alternative tricky angle used by women on occasion, where it would seem to have obtained a superior sexual appetite towards her man. I'm saying she's ready for love making all day long. Everyday there's a day. Pretty much nothing is off limits, and she has the body of a woman but the dirty mind of a man. If that is the case, there's a chance that man could be involved with a lady whose strategy is to win a trip down the aisle by believing what he desires is having "committed sex" with her.

Now committed sex is a mirage. It may look like regular sex, touch like regular sex, and many times even feel like happy, intense, glorified sex. But just look a little closer and you can identify the difference. With normal regular sex, both parties are satisfied and pleased to the point of acceptance. During committed sex, however, only one party can be satisfied to where the other may seem left out sexually and feel obligated to perform sexual acts. Women may allow themselves in that predicament because they either feel if they're not sexually involved with their partner, then someone else will come in and satisfy them, or their partner will just leave them entirely. So, against their own judgement, these females will convince themselves into unfulfilling sexual circumstances in hopes their partner will get that they want and, in a way, return the favor with long term monogamy and security. Earlier in my life, I had real trouble deciphering the good and bad behaviors of sex. I will say that paying attention to body language really helped put under a microscope the tell-tale signs. If she gives off any resistance or hesitation like the rolling of her eyes or a deep sigh, the shaking of her head even at the discussion of sex. Those examples could be indicators that she's not interested, either in the moment or at all getting involved sexually. It may seem obvious, reading these examples, to be able to notice this issue, but you would be amazed how little we as men are aware when we tunnel vision towards sex. See spot run. Spot run fast. Run spot run. I learned as I grew and got older; it's an exceedingly difficult conversation to have with women, discussing her reservations and concerns with this type of issue because they believe those dialogues will cause rifts or even break ups. So many women will tend to play ball in a way and go with the flow, hoping those moments of committed sex will be few and far in-between.

The four Cs to a relationship are compromise, consistency, commitment and, the most important one to me, communication. How can you ever share what you want the most with the other person knowing, without expressing yourself verbally? Written notes and assumptions fail to register because they have no tone. To this day, it's the only question that even after reading books on communication and engaging in social interactions with people on this exact topic, I find no universal answer. Yes, talking things out can lead to arguments and disagreements. Fights pursue, breakups occur, and sometimes even marriages end. But that happens regardless. Any trash not taken out starts to smell. I understand. Avoid all problems at all costs but trust me, the committed sex only lasts for so long before problems occur anyway. She'll either gain resentment towards her man for feeling he "made" her feel she had to have sex with him to keep him happy or she will just get tired of that way of living and move on to another situation that she feels is less demanding.

There's no perfect solution to this problem, only perfect expectations. A man can only decide what works best for him and his own circumstances. It's better to be with someone who wants to be with you, other than the one who just wants to be. Insert name next to girlfriend, wife, friend, you name it. I know having someone is better than having no one, but if that person really isn't interested in being involved with you completely, you're alone anyway. You may not feel it, but soon you'll see it. It's all just a matter of **Time.**

VIII.

Puppy Love is Real Love

My mom is beautiful. No, I'm serious. You know how most people, when asked about their mothers' physical appearance, will describe them the same way. Beautiful. I realize it's common verbiage for kids to refer to their mom, but when it's subject to my momma, it's absolute fact. Sometimes, I believe selfishly, my mom was created on this planet just to raise me. I really admire her for her internal and external beauty. Understand, if you had a mom like me, you would have no problem feeling the exact same way. The woman's story was almost fairy tale like. Allow me to explain.

See, my mom made a conscious decision to wait around till she found her version of Prince Charming, which at first attempt at storytelling, my dad was not to her. His glasses, the way he tried and failed with those lame mack daddy lines over the phone. A very funny story to hear. But as most Hollywood romantic comedies eventually go, through time and perseverance, he won her undying heart and they became husband and wife. High school sweethearts turned family hustle. One man, one love, one life. Yes, of course that's my mother's story and how her life turned out. In retrospect, it was a pretty good move because my father was not a bad man to be with at all. But I cannot make an entire point based off one premier isolated example. That's called **the exception,** which I briefly described in the beginning of the book. If you also remember from earlier pages, I make my statements and prove my theories by highlighting **the rule** a.k.a. the many. With that being said, yes, I understand not all high school sweethearts who get married stay that way or even last very long. I have read somewhere that close to half of all marriages in the United States end in divorce.

Now that we've gotten all of that out of the way, let's focus on the why. I'm not a scientist or even a marriage counselor. Just an extremely observant man who doesn't need glasses to see things that are the obvious. I knew a girl in high school who looked at dating as catching the plague. She hated it. Nothing about being with a guy, holding hands, kissing, and, of course, most of all, sex gave her the slightest taste of excitement. For three years, I thought she was gay. She had guys she was friends with just never on a romantic level. Fortunately, for her sake and mine, because our everyday disputes about why being in a relationship was pointless compared to eternal bliss were to the point of wearing me out, at last she found her male match. He was equally pessimistic towards love and dating. To that, the love gods had other plans. So, the two ended up together. It was swift and actually kind of cool to look at. Everything that couple represented and displayed about stereotypical newlywed couples and public signs of affection, became their own personal battle cries. He held her hand, she kissed his cheek. They even put their hands in each other's jeans back pockets like in the movies. What more could I say about them two? It was a classic Dr. Jekyll, Mr. Hyde social experiment gone right. She even told me some months later, that she believed she loved him. Now I can't stress enough how against romance this young lady was. She was the type of girl that threw pudding cups at couples that kissed in the cafeteria. I mean that's just how much she despised love. Was it because deep down she yearned for that same type of love and affection? In any other case I would say sure, of course, no problem. But not this girl. She simply hated couples and everything they stood for, so hearing her use words like "love" was about as foreign as another language to me. So, the day she called me crying saying her and her "Fathead," which was the nickname she blessed him with, had just broken up and that she hates love again. Most other girls declare that on a regular basis, especially moments right after a huge breakup, but in this instance it's different. If I had ever thought that this girl was against love and the concept of being involved in love before, then consider this situation Armageddon.

To make a long story short, of course she moved on and eventually had other relationships with men, even had children. But it wasn't made from love. More so spite. What I mean by that is that girl turned woman was stricken by the menacing "first love hurt" and never fully recovered. I know you can talk to a single woman with how she feels about relationships and love with marriage with her, getting into this dark cloud and upsetting story. Explaining men's faults and why being with one is detrimental, causing nothing but heartache and pain. Every man knows at least one woman like that. But you ever took a moment and sat back to think why she even got to this point in her life? See, women are life elephants. Wait. Not like that. You know the old saying, elephants don't forget anything. I don't know who came up with that. I have never seen an elephant up close or anything or did a study on memory or the repetitive nature of an elephant but it's a saying nonetheless, so just roll with me. Women don't forget anything. They can remember things that happened to them fifty years ago that essentially had nothing to do with you and seemingly, out of nowhere, allow that moment to anger them and tend to lash out at the closest person to them with no warning or signal. That also applies to relationship memory. You ever thought how a woman even knows to guard her heart or emotions when it applies to a guy? Or why a female is even hesitant to pursue something with a man even when she really likes him? Well, before you get to the end of her story, it's wise to date back to the beginning of a girl's dating history. I promise you, just about every girl's very first boyfriend could tell you there was very little restraint towards making her his girl. I mean how could there be? How do you know you're supposed to protect your feelings if they never needed protection to begin with?

Consider someone driving for the very first time. Never rode in a car before nor has anyone in the entire world teaching or telling them anything about a car or the procedure for how to drive one. Every single action involving the car would be a brand new exciting experience. The opening of the door and getting inside is a thrill. Putting on a seatbelt and hearing the click as the seat holds in place is an adventure. The adjusting of the mirrors, the holding of the keys, putting the key into the ignition, and the initial turn to start the engine. All must be exhilarating events for this person seeing and feeling all of this for the first time in life. How strange would it be to tell this person not to drive too fast in the rain or you'll slide off the road, or to look both ways at an intersection even if you have the right of way to continue because a wreck can occur? That person would have a slew of questions to ask pertaining to all the new information you just installed into his or her life.

For instance, the young lady I mentioned earlier, who had a true distaste for relationships or anybody who was in one. I told you how she finally got into a relationship but failed to disclose how fast and abruptly the relationship glued together. It was fast. It was one day she met him, the next day she liked him. The day after that, they were talking on the phone. The day after that, he was her number one friend on her top five on myspace. Yeah, I said it. Myspace. Remember that? The social media site that, at one time, was even cooler than Facebook? The next day, Boom. Boyfriend and girlfriend. Five days. Now you may be telling yourself, "Wow that was fast to be involved with someone you haven't known long," right? Well, compared to what? To her, it was right on time. Every action and step she took towards the boy were new and exciting. All she wanted was more of those same feelings. So, just like a person who does drugs for the first time in their life, feeling that incredible high must be amazing. So amazing that a repeated action soon follows. I'm sure that's how drug addicts become addicted. If the high wasn't like anything they've ever had, there wouldn't be such a change of mindset on how much urgency gets placed on the next one. Feelings are powerful. First time feelings are even more powerful than that. It's the incredible emotions you get that block the part of the brain that triggers restraint and is wary to move forward with something. The girl I knew from high school just wanted to enjoy the new and pleasing feelings she would get from being around and thinking about her boyfriend. The more she thought about him, the more excited she got. It's a natural, normal feeling. It is a feeling that should be experienced more often but unfortunately, life events occur and then decisions are made. As the first love can bring a true high like no other, that first heartbreak can devastate just as much. It creates pain to the point that it becomes the center point and total focus of a woman's thoughts through relationships in general. Let's refer to the car analogy from earlier. I explained that if a person who never drove or rode in a car before or was never told about automobiles ever, would be unlikely to have a negative thought process towards the driving experience. They would probably drive with reckless abandon, like running through stop signs, jumping through speed bumps. Maybe even attempt to drive backwards like in the James Bond movies. Who knows? It's the rush of excitement and adrenaline of a new fresh experience that would have this new driver just enjoying the time behind the wheel. Right up until their very first crash or unfortunate circumstance occurs. Just as exciting and joyful the feeling of driving for the very first time would be, the pain and horror from the wreck shares the same reversal impact. The more hurt the person would feel from the event, the more traumatized the life is now. Some people can get into car crashes and bounce right back into the driver's seat as soon as their able to.

Take for instance NASCAR racers. I'm sure their first crashes are very dramatic experiences; laced with quick, shooting thoughts of quitting and pursuits of other possible fulfilling endeavors. But then, like the great Ricky Bobby from the classic movie *Talladega Nights: The Ballad of Ricky Bobby,* those racers rise up from the ashes like a phoenix and realize racing is their true passion and livelihood, get the wreck out of their memory, jump back into those speed machines, and continue their purpose. It takes a strong mindset to move on from hurt and painful events in your life. I remember the first time I got really hurt from playing football. Prior to that injury, I received little nicks and bruises here and there, but nothing serious. This time was different though. It was a shot to my knee and as I fell my knee began to give out and the pain tricked me into believing I knew it was going to simply break off and fall on the field. The initial thought was my knee was gone and that notion alone sent shock waves throughout my entire body. Scared me to death. Only once my coach and doctors came to me and lifted me up, that I realized my knee was still attached to my leg and I was able to walk. After some treatment, later in the game I could limp. Then two weeks later, I could run and by the end of the season, I was flying. I never even remembered the fact I cried like a baby because I thought I had become a pirate and needed a wooden leg.

It's not the pain of the breakup or how hurtful the first relationship that dictates how a female will be afterwards with men. It's how she handles and moves on from that painful experience that shapes her attitude towards the next relationship and so on. Women do a fantastic job of what I call "crutch learning". When you see a person just getting out of the hospital and they are still in a large amount of pain, due to a hurt leg or lower body injury, they're usually permitted to crutches; which are basically used to keep a person upright and help support their balance. While you happen to see some people hop and jump forward, forcing their crutches to keep up with their forward momentum, others limp and lean on their crutches, forcing the medical equipment to take the lead and direct the person's movements, moving forward. In a restricting kind of way, it's a reason to justify future actions with remorse and sometimes even pity. It's a tolerated behavior that we as men have allowed because we never really focused on the injury, but how good the girl looks limping. I'm not saying a woman who's been hurt can't love and that love be real. A woman can still love and care for a man even after her first love ends abruptly and it be genuine, passionate, and worthy of commitment. My point is that it lacks originality.

I had a debate with a woman I worked with one time about love and energy. The conversation demonstrated women giving one hundred percent of themselves in a relationship until they were uninvested or uninterested in that relationship to where then, that energy goes to zero. Then, refuel up to the next relationship with a recharged one hundred percent. My co-worker simply told me that is possible due to a simple fact that women just can love harder than men, which I agreed with to a certain point. What I come to believe is what I've been told my entire life. Is that **women choose to love, and men fall in love.** That's simply because women rarely get into relationships with men initially with no excitement or desire for something long standing with absolute success. On the other hand, I've seen men add girlfriends like Pokémon cards, where they would divide up energy based on who they liked more, until something clicked and emotional attachment confided in them, forcing them to make a leading decision with one. It may not always be the most rational decision making, but hey we're men, and just like the commercial said about the cereal applejacks, we eat what we like. In the end, love is love. That idea has been the biggest concept I've had the most struggle with accepting. I had to decide that if a woman is loving me, I run with it. Whether it's her first or hundredth time loving. The fact that you can get a woman to show absolutely any encouraging emotion after an emotional car crash is even more satisfying. Of course, we would rather, as men, a woman with little to no scarring, but if the outcome is what you hoped for, then the journey there is a side footnote.

The BAR

The more sexual partners a woman has, the higher the bar goes up on her greatest sexual experience. For example, if out of five guys, the fifth guy is her greatest experience, then the fifth guy becomes the bar and the sixth and up person is compared to him, until someone replaces that greatest experience, making that the new bar. If a married virgin never has any other experience other than her husband, then she's married to her "default bar" to where sexual commitment is easier due to the lack of knowledge and experience with other men. Only curiosity and wonder exist. Experience does not.

Don't Know, Don't Really Care

Take the blockbuster movie *Twilight*. The intense romantic exchange between Bella and Edward is the symbol of how the first love dictates decision making. How I can determine whether Bella has never been in any love before or not is immensely obvious. The complete lack of awareness and disregard for identifying red flags is the dead giveaway. Edward tried to ward Bella off countless times with graphic depictions of his violent behavior, lifestyle, and a murderous filled past. Yet, Bella not only dodged the warnings but at times seemed more drawn to the danger. In fact, throughout the course of the movie, the more dangerous and deadly the circumstances became, the stronger the love connection to Edward Bella has. It was simply due to there being no other time in Bella's young life she could recall there being such strong emotional feelings towards someone before. It was the feelings Bella felt toward Edward that grew so strong and felt so comforting that it became apparent that the young lady never in her life wanted to not have those feelings in her life again. It was the connection to Edward that Bella associated her newly filled heart with. So, no matter the initial danger or risk involved, Bella would stay with Edward. Point blank period. There's no pain to compare to. No fear of loss to remind her of. Just new exciting feelings and the commitment to those feelings no matter the outcome.

IX.

Entitlement Misuse

Life is funny, man. It's amazing how much you can actually learn just from living life. My dad used to tell me all the time, "Life will show you some things that I can't." Which is the truth. Everything I ever wanted to know, understand and learn, the majority of the information received simply come from being alive and experiencing everyday life. People that I sit with and have deep meaningful conversations with, ask me from time to time for advice. Whether it pertains to love, family or even just managing yourself in general. I used to try and produce these memorable quotes that sounded like they could be applied to a bumper sticker or t-shirt, like my dad would. And I quickly learned that was not really my gift. So, I just found to keep it simple and direct when giving people words of wisdom. One, because I'm not a life guru and secondly, why people ask me for advice to this day, is still a pretty weird concept. Just because I don't believe I've lived or experienced enough to be certified in that department. Nonetheless, I still get repeatedly asked so I simply just tell people two words that personally mean the most to the shaping of my life thus far. Those words being, "**Don't Die**." It's about as honest and genuine I can be with a person without becoming all Gandhi or Dr. Martin Luther King on them. In addition, I believe you can apply that phrase to any and every aspect of life. Whether you want to learn about, no matter what circumstance presents itself. Just don't die and I'm more than sure you will figure it out eventually.

I was giving this little nugget of truth to a man I was having a conversation within a Burger King one day. I had just picked up my tray with my order of chicken fries and a side of regular fries along with a medium chocolate shake because I was watching my weight, just trying to be healthy. You know, taking care of the temple. That's when I observed a young man sitting by the window in the corner all by himself which just seemed odd. Not because he was alone in a corner booth at a Burger King, but because he was the only one in the dining area alone in a corner booth. So, just like in the movies, he was deep sighing and glazing out of the window like he was trying to reenact a TV commercial for depression or something. The only thing that was missing from this scene was it raining outside with the Usher "Let it Burn" track playing in the background and the setting would be finalized. Now me being at the time the friendly neighborhood Spiderman and always looking for an opportunity to gather information to apply for my own life, I approached him. Once I got close enough for him to temporarily get out of his deep emotional connection with his own unhappiness, I saw the perfect opportunity to try out my newly found phrase on him.

So, with expectancy mixed with overenthusiasm, I about yelled out, "Hey man, just don't die. It'll be all good."

It sounded just as dumb as it reads to you right now. He almost jumped out of the booth, which scared us both because even though I assume I may give off a comforting friendly warm vibe when I talk to people, I must continually remind myself that everybody in the world may not want to be my personal guinea pig for research.

Fortunately for me, after his initial shock from the misuse of my catchphrase, he calmly responded with a very monotone "I'm not trying to kill myself, I'm fine."

Yes. Advice slogan zero, people I offered it to that didn't work, one. He did offer me to sit and eat with him, which was unexpected due to my verbal sack fumble, but welcomed. I did sit with this gentleman and to my surprise he opened to telling me his whole reasoning he was in the fast-food lobby all alone. The guy wasn't depressed. He was bored and lonely, which I completely understood and related to. He told me about his situation with his girlfriend and about how she constantly yelled at and argued with him on a regular basis. Never once letting up with battling his manhood, by comparing him to what she felt a "real man" is and what a "real man" would do in every situation. How he couldn't understand how it seemed nothing he did was ever good enough, yet his girlfriend seemed content with staying with him by never threatening to leave him or pursue other opportunities with these other so called "real men". I reassured him by running through every situation that I've shared his position. How I've felt inadequate with some females due to the fact they were constantly disapproving of how I conducted myself and how poorly of a job I was managing business. Treating them like the queens that they always reminded by social media were.

See, women are just as smart as they are dumb and what I mean by that is simply, they don't just do things just to do them. They have a reasoning for everything. Whether the decisions are reasonable or not, they are rarely based off emotions. A lot of times these choices may blow up in their faces, but that same decision can be repeated in a cycle. Hence the term, smart slash dumb. My new friend at the Burger King still looked confused. He told me that women want a good man and that was what he tried to be. His mentality was to do good and good will be done back to you. Which I completely agree with, but then explained to him that it's not the act that is persuasive, it's how the act is received that tells the story.

See, here's the smart with women. One thing a woman knows, is the man she's dealing with. Women know what their man is capable of. You know the saying, "if you knew better, you'd do better," right? Well, there you go. A female understands that if a man could do better than her, he would have been with her already. She knows your ceiling. She understands her limitations. Your girlfriend can see what kind of women you can get just from being around you for five minutes. So, her decision for choosing you is simply based on her competitive spirit or lack thereof.

I knew a young lady in her twenties living in New Orleans. Her parents should have named her, "Good Lord" because that's what you said every time you see her. Long silky black hair down her back, light green eyes, cocoa skin, luscious lips, and a booty made from the heavens. All natural. Which only matters today because sometimes it's hard to pick a real woman from a sex doll. Can I get an amen? I'm telling you, this was the type of woman that had NBA wife written all over her forehead. Which brings up my next point, because this young goddess had an absolute love hate relationship with professional athletes. She dated football players, a basketball player, and even a baseball player. All to no avail. I mean her dating life took more Ls than any team Lebron James played for then leaves.

I was privileged enough to see her in a bar downtown one day and just had to ask her," Girl, why in the world do you continually date these ball players knowing it's more than likely going to end in heartbreak?"

It was like a question that slapped her in the face because she sat up in her bar stool, turned to me as those emerald green eyes that glistening in the dim lighting of the bar started welling up with tear water. She told me what registers to me even today. She told me she understood that it was a challenge being with those type of men and that most of them were simply just looking for sex from her, which she agreed to, with the hopes that she could then after show herself more than just a sexual object to the man with time, affection and anything else to convince him that she's worthy of commitment. At first, it seemed unusual to hear this take of action from a woman with so much to offer. College educated, independent, available, and did I mention her booty? Ok, just checking. So why in the world would she continually attack this brick wall when even statistics reveal the odds are stacked against her? She told me she has a friend that married a ball player and that they have this seemingly secure, beautiful life with the house in the hills, chopped full of comfort and enjoyment. Before she could even go on telling the rest of the story, my inquisitive light bulb went off. It's not about what this lady feels she deserves, it's about what she feels she deserves based on her friend she sized herself up next to. Here is the dumb part. There is a great t-shirt saying, "seeing is believing". It is not what a woman believes she is capable of that drives her toward a certain relation or situation, it's the example that she witnesses herself that confirms is possible and worth pursuing, or at the very least, worth striving for.

I used to drive past a church every Sunday on my way to work. This church looked like any other church except the parking lot was unique. That's why it always caught my eye every Sunday I drove past it. In the front of this church, it had two big blue signs that read "Pastor" on one and "First Lady" on the other. Each sign attained its own reserved parking space where two separate Mercedes-Benzes were in those spaces. From a distance it seems like no big deal, they have churches where the pastor and his wife drive luxury vehicles and park in the front of the buildings so no biggie. In this case, however, it was not the two cars that caused my eyes to give the parking lot so much attention. It was the entire first and second row of parking spots that were filled with Mercedes Benzes that had me staring. Same styles, mostly the same colors and same years made. Now, I'm sure that church didn't have that many pastors and first ladies. Couldn't be, not by a long shot. So why all those Benzes in the parking lot parked right up front next to the pastor and his wife's cars? Simple, seeing is believing. I've been to quite a few churches in my life and have seen many different sets of pastors and pastor's wives. Not one I've met looked like anybody in particular. No movie stars, supermodels, nothing like that, just your run-of-the-mill, nice friendly folks. They could be your next-door neighbor, schoolteacher, or principal. And that's the thought process for a lot of people. If I look like them, walk like them, talk like them and work like them, who's to say I can't live like them? Drive cars like them. They are no better than me. If they can do it, so can I.

Now let's switch hands. Why not apply that same attitude towards being a professional athlete or C.E.O. of a social media juggernaut like Facebook? That's easy. The mentality is I'm not six foot eight, run a four point three in the forty-yard dash and can't dunk a basketball. Facebook is already established, I'm not smart enough and I don't know anybody in that field. We talk like that. Women tend to live like that regarding men. I'm not beautiful, I'm not curvy, professional athletes don't approach me, none of my friends have successful relationships with ball players, plus, what would a guy like that want with a girl like me? All it takes is a change in one of those realities. Just one relatable example and the entire mind frame of how a woman perceives herself and her options instantly change. If she can do it and I'm on her level, then it's attainable for me.

So, let's reverse back to the conversation I was having with my buddy at Burger King going through his thunderstorm night in the middle of the day. Remember how he told me that his girlfriend didn't respect him as a man and constantly bagged his ability to please her, but yet never made a move upward to a man she valued more?

Well, I asked him. "How did the guys she dated before you treat her? Has she ever shared any successful past relationship stories?"

He thought about it for a moment, drew a Joker type smile and then almost laughed aloud and replied, "No, all of her past boyfriends cheated on her and treated her poorly. Yes, they spoiled her and bought her material things, but the relationships never lasted with her longer than a year or so."

But right after that confession, the soloist in the restaurant dining room took a breath, exhaled, and slowly drew out, "But that still doesn't answer why she is so ungrateful with me. Why doesn't she appreciate me and love me more than she has in our relationship thus far?"

I was waiting for that question since he conveyed his issue with his girlfriend to me; like a mouse waiting for the refrigerator door to open so it could make its way to the piece of cheese that made its way to the bottom of the door just sitting there ready for the taking.

With a warm smile and full heart, I simply asked, "How many times have you gotten her what she asked for in this relationship?"

He replied, "Almost every time."

"And how many times has she complained still?"

"Same answer. Every time."

"What about the times your manhood was tested? How many times did you leave her after that?"

He gave me the deer in the headlights look as if his brain exploded after being asked the chess move question. His answer?

"None. Never."

I said, "Exactly. You didn't leave just like other men before you never left. That woman will leave you before you ever leave her. That's why she refuses to change, she was never given any reason to. Being with her felt like Déjà vu. Same song different verse. She chooses you because you remind her of what she knows she's capable of. Another security blanket."

It's important to remind yourself that the truth can and will simply set you free. Changes in patterns can be a positive thing when dealing with a woman in an extremely comfortable predicament. It persuades a woman to take ownership of her actions. To change what's, she's used to and also who's she's used to. **You can influence, persuade, convince even bribe, but you cannot make someone do anything.** For women, it's all about experiences and moments. For men, it's all about success and failures. The young man I was having this deep and insightful conversation with, located in a corner booth next to a window, in a Burger King lobby, alone at four in the afternoon, finished his food, thanked me for the talk, dumped his tray and walked out of the restaurant, leaving me alone with my thoughts, just as he was before I walked up to him a brief time before.

As I took a long drag from my soda, that now tasted like colored soda water from all the ice in my cup that had melted, a woman from the register at the front counter yelled out to me, "Hey, I was listening to your conversation with that guy who was crying before you walked in. You should write a book."

I asked for a pen, grabbed a napkin, and decided to write down everything I remembered from the talk I just had. Life is funny man. It's amazing how much you can learn from just living life.

X.

I Guess I'll See You Next Lifetime

When I decided to write this book, I first had to make a personal choice. The way to go that route was simple. I had to ask myself some questions. How honest was I going to be in this book? How personal and transparent would I allow myself to be in my writing? I can't stress that statement enough that I'm no therapist or counselor, at all. Sometimes, I honestly believe I have the same number of emotional moments as most people would like to admit, I'm human. Yet, no medication or treatment will be needed to regulate or even stabilize my thoughts or emotional process. Because my treatment was to be as real and honest as I could to keep the integrity of this book pure enough, so men and I'm sure some curious women who read this will no matter what they believe, will never question how legitimate and true this book is. That is something you can live with, regardless of opinion. Saying all of that leads into this. Growing up how I thought didn't bother me. I was always a pretty positive person when it came to girls and potential girlfriends. I held hands, I kissed, I went on dates. I had few restrictions from sharing my feelings and wants, because I believed back then when it came to love and dating, you got back what you gave. My interactions with females were consistent. I'd meet the girl I liked, get the phone number from the girl I liked and would be poised to end up on dates with the girl I liked. It was that simple. Normal transitions throughout life. But, if you come to live and learn, if every situation went that way every time for everyone, there would be no purpose for this book to exist. Normality rarely gets published. Irregularities win gold medals. There were early indications that interactions with females were set up for matrix like moments. Most of those signs were ignored up until recently once I became aware of my life and hit my fork in the road. I realized I was shallow. Not the shallowest person there is in life, but shallow nonetheless. Physical appearance has always been the driving force for my selections regarding female companions. Any person who knows me well would agree. Some would disagree with me but yes, I believe men are hooked on looks first. I would go as far to say a woman's exterior is a major deciding factor towards a man's choosing. That could be a major reason why so many beauty products and fashion lines push their respectable labels down women's throats from an early age. Promoting how well a woman looks on the outside, the more men like myself will approach them. It wasn't so much the pretty face that carried the case for me as it was the curvaceous nature of the female anatomy. It was the foundation of how I even viewed girls when I was younger. Of course, you grow up and mature as you develop as a man wanting different attributes from women. Still, a shapely woman is the on switch for motivational support for me. It's what I wanted, always wanted, and would have to take something supernatural to change that.

I digress, that's not the meaning of this chapter though, where I was planning to transition to once I talked the girl crazy phase I went through that became the base of my desire for them. I'm not a huge fan of horoscopes. How your birthday and sign with the shape of the moon and stars can dictate the type of person you are and who you do and don't match well with. Only because the accuracy is scary on point. Still, I'm not a big fan. One curious day, however, I was stopped in the mall by a woman who had a table set up giving people horoscope card readings. I've heard of tarot card readings but horoscope cards? Never heard of that and that was the trap that drew me in. In addition to that, this lady was set up in the open, in front of a Footlocker.; not slid down a dark alley with dim lighting, guarded by black cats all while horror music was playing in the background. So, with an open mind, I proceeded to sit down with the fortune teller and answered all her questions with truth and honesty. The pretty fortune teller with a soft voice and kind spirit, proceeded to tell me that I was a very visual person with attention to detail. And my wants and desires will drive me towards success, but will also attract much pain and suffering. She was that accurate. Gives me goosebumps to this day thinking about that encounter with that lady. I believe God sent her to give me that message. I had never seen her before or since that day.

I had my burning bush moment at an early age. Before then, I was completely unaware of understanding foreshadowing. But as a man, it's right as rain. I'm a man of consistency. A man of simple patterns. I tend to blanket myself in a regular daily routine. Call me an A, B, C, D guy. I love stability. It gives me comfort. All the more reason the inconsistencies in my romantic life was so interesting to me. Since I was a teenager, my encounters with females would all tend to roll the same way as dice. I would tend to run in a certain female and right away, I'm crushing. I would instantly put females in three separate boxes to how I receive them in my life. The first box is the girlfriend box. I would see a girl I thought was really attractive and automatically see us dating and would try to figure out how to woo her into a relationship. As soon as I met her, she instantly became a priority. The second box was the sex box. Self-explanatory. Not attractive enough for a relationship but oddly, enough for a sexual encounter. Most of the time the decision was based off reputation and if my friends already slept with her or not. Hey, like I said, I was young and had some figuring out to do. It's all part of the process. The third box was the buddy box. Not attractive enough for a relationship nor a sexual one but intriguing enough for a friendship. As a man, you can guess that box was pretty small. Most of the women I wasn't physically attracted to, I didn't show much care to, unless they did have an amazing personality or shared a trait that aligned to the woman I really wanted. I found little need for friendship from females back in the day. Again, the maturity tree was in its sprouting phase. Far from fully grown. That's just who I was.

Now, here comes the soap opera. Let's say I end up speaking to the girl I chose for the girlfriend box. The next steps would go as follows, I talk to her, she says I'm a great guy, I ask her out, she says yes, the day comes, she flakes. I called to find out the meaning for the denial, but I got no answer. A week to a month goes by. I find out she's talking to a new guy. They're a couple and I still get no explanation or closure to why things started off great with this woman, only to end that way. I always say, the hardest questions to get answered are the whys. I believe it's the most difficult to receive or to comprehend mostly because of the hurt behind the why you end up gaining.

A special connection with a woman means a lot to a man, so feelings get damaged when the special feeling isn't reciprocated back from the woman. Just like in the movie *HER* when Scarlett Johansson tells the main character Joaquin Phoenix that she is in love with thousands of other men.

Towards this issue, I was incredibly open to the why. So, I could make proper adjustments and change this unforgiving pattern for the better. It reminded me of the movie *Hitch* where the main character played by Will Smith (and not to spoil the movie but come on. Who hasn't seen *Hitch*?) has his own growing pains when it pertains to the game of love. He initially pushes too hard towards his first serious girlfriend. Showing all his emotion and love in a short amount of time. Ultimately pushing her away and she instantly being involved with another guy very quickly. He finds out the most painful way possible. In the act of his former love and the new rebound engaged in each other. The scene is set up in the rain, all the more symbolizing for the protagonist who asked the most important question,

"Why?" After the encounter, the main character Hitch becomes a more aware and strategic dater by protecting his heart with his blueprint of gaming women with logic and discipline. Believing that if you go about living with premeditated feelings, you can never get hurt. But as you watch the rest of that great classic, you find his strategy with love loses purpose. What I took from the dramatic rain scene in the movie was that through the heartbreak in the moment the main character was aware enough to ask his why and accepted the truthful answer. That motivated him to take action with the proper steps to rewire his attitude with women in the future.

In my similar experiences in the dating world, I was spared the answers I needed for change, or at least closure. Instead of the women giving their why it didn't work out and what I could have done to have possibly made the situation work out. I would be prone to receive the simplest most cliché possible. That's right, you guessed it. "It's not you, it's me." The first few times, yeah sure I would accept that reply. I didn't know any better but after a while those answers did little to problem solve for me. The response no longer had any sufficient reasoning behind it. Just a simple cop out as I took it. Sometime later, after I got older and those same females that once felt those other men in their lives provided more purpose for them as opposed to me were now calling me and messaging on social media, it convinced me otherwise. One by one, year after year, I'm now being told by these same women after time has passed that I was truly the catch. They're taking a full out assault of pursing my time, affection and most important, my commitment. Which at that time had me confused. Where in the world was this energy of attachment coming from? One day, I'm nothing more than a pumpkin to these ladies, but months and years later I Cinderella into the Belle of the ball?

It sent me into a detective state of searching for knowledge and understanding towards the psychology behind women and these behaviors. I realize that so far, this chapter seems like a case of the young man blues.

Most guys I grew up with had all experienced their own individual shares of hurt and disappointment when it comes to dealing with relationships and women. I wasn't born last night. What man hasn't pursued a female, started the dating process and even reached the optimistic phase of a love connection, all to have these hopes smashed into a million pieces once a female gives the ol' "give and go" by showing all the right signs; having you, as a man, believing she's interested,   then without any warning leaves with no real reasoning why. I get it. It happens to the best of us. It could even be a slight reach saying those experiences helped guys to develop into better, stronger men today, when it deals with overcoming tough, sudden obstacles involving everyday life. It wasn't until I reached my thirties that I started to see my circumstances as unique. I sat down at my table one day, grabbed a pen and a sheet of paper and wrote down every girl, every year I met I wanted a relationship with. Wrote every scenario to why it failed. Then, like when you stare at a word search puzzle and the words start to just pop out at you, I saw a repetitive connection with my romantic disconnections. Like clockwork, every year since I was twenty-five to the time, I started writing it all down to the present day, which was a little over seven years. I saw two women I met in which I was interested. One at the beginning of the summer and the other at the end of the year. Every year for seven years. It was strange. I dug even deeper and wrote down where I was at the time in my life. Living conditions, salary, body type, car model, everything I could think of that could influence a woman's choosing, or in my case, not choosing.

What could I have done to sway the pendulum in my favor? What was my part in this lost pursuit of love? What did I do wrong? Why could I have no problem with women I didn't want to pursue anything with, but the ones I pursued frustrated me the most? Was I a young Hitch, just pushing too hard forcing these females away? If I did everything so wrong or wasn't the right one for them, then why were these women calling and pursing me now? Years later and a few months after. My life hasn't changed very much. The money I made was about the same. I wasn't any more loving or caring than I was when I was after them. Same man, same life. It was hard figuring things out. Hard until I had access to video chat and enhanced camera phones.

I was seeing the answers all those years and just never paid any attention to the test I was taking. See, my life didn't change but theirs did. Drastically. Their lives changed physically, emotionally, financially, and not practically for the better. These ladies were mere shadows of themselves. Unidentifiable to me even at first glance. A Facebook page once filled with beautiful, flawless faces. Dressed with wall punching, fist biting outfits confirmed by hundreds even thousands of likes and thirst emojis. Mirroring the lifestyles of extremely happy, seemingly fulfilled, world dominating women. These profiles were now kidnapped and replaced by dull, sad, uninterested, unrecognizable women. Filled with baby pictures, followed by awkward poses at bars and daquiri shops. A plethora of high school photos with the taglines hashtag throwback that were posted every day that week and even on weekends. Selfies that started from the chest up. I got it. I figured it out. I realized I had become the result of the process of elimination game these women were now playing. These were the women that no longer controlled the attention of every man from simply checking the mailbox or walking down the street. This was the nonverbal explanations I was able to piece together from lack of answers given from my female counterparts. I still got what I needed to devise a portal theory. It's like women lived two lives.

A woman explained to me one day that **beauty IS the beast**. Being beautiful is the same punishment as the reward. Beauty can become a blinder to the path one is truly destined for. I know that women do try in part to be the best they can be, by making the best choices that they can. Unfortunately, because some women are given different opportunities from others, different choices are made. When women I've known looked their best, they made their worst decisions. Ironically though, when they would then look their worst, they made the best decisions possible. You can't tell a beautiful twenty-year-old anything, but a single thirty-five-year-old with three kids will hear what you have to say. The humility of life is a fascinating ordeal. There are two game changers in a female's life. Aging and body change. Picture a world class sprinter training for the Olympics. The runner gets positioned into the blocks and waits for the gun to go off to run.

The sprint coach runs up to the Olympic hopeful and says, "Wait, aren't you going to stretch out and warm up before you just start running full speed?"

The sprinter replies with an overconfident grin and replies back, "Hey coach, relax. I won the world championships without stretching or getting warm. Why would the Olympics be any different?"

If the racer doesn't ever pull a muscle while running, nothing in the routine will ever tend to change. But once that hamstring pops and the racers career never truly recovers back to its award-winning form. The thought process of the sprinter changes immediately from I can do what I want, to stretching and warming up is life. Take youth and beauty as the hamstring and the injury as aging and poor decisions along the way. My dad would always tell me growing up that there are three types of people in the world. People who learn from their own mistakes, people who learn from other people's mistakes and people who keep making the same mistakes over and over again. Life is the world's greatest teacher. Some lessons are just harsher than others and when it comes to women and choosing men, it shows in their faces who chooses well and who's just waiting to stop choosing and simply be chosen. But by then, the choice for that no longer is theirs. The choice becomes the man's and women don't like becoming that choice.

XI.

In the Meantime…

I'm bad with days and weeks. My Mondays run into my Fridays and my weeks all feel like one long one. But, I'm extremely aware of months and years if that makes any sense. If something happens to me one particular day, in that exact moment, I can feel and comprehend the time and revel in it. A few days after that event, even a week or so, that time that pasts become ancient. When it comes to years, however, everything is in plain sight. Me and my little sister are seven years apart. I graduated from high school eighteen years ago and Juvenile's classic hit "Back That Azz Up" is twenty-four years old. Why I remember years clearer than any other period of time somehow makes perfect sense to me. Years determine the longest amount of change in one particular amount of time. Yes, you can grow in one day. Develop enormous amounts of growth in weeks. Progress significantly in months. But years reflect the foundation of who you are. The extension of the home just represents how much that foundation allowed growth. Go back to the time when you graduated college or studied abroad for even just a short or large amount of time. How your friends and family saw you when you left. Now remember when you returned home, and your same family saw you then. How did they react? Did they still recognize you? Did they express how different you looked and how much you changed to them? But to you, it's all the same. No big deal. You look in the mirror and see the same old you. That's what years can do. Considerable time goes by, you engage in many things, but it seems little time has passed, and you haven't accomplished much.

Now, apply that notion to a person's social life. More specifically, a single person's social life. If there's one thing I know if nothing else, I know how to be single. Not purposely though. I always told people when asked if I were single or not, I would always joke, "I'm single by default." It sounded funny but at that point in my life, it was not a game. Not only would I strike out with dates and hangout sessions, I had historic dry spells. There were times I could remember going six to eight months in a year without having sex. Trust me, if you've gone that long without any sexual activity while pursuing sexual activity, one can only imagine how disgusting the web history on your phone and laptop would look like. Still wouldn't be as bad as mine. So don't feel that bad. And that was me, not dating much and little to no sex. But when that drought would end, I would try my best to make up for lost time. So, in the end that was my dating career. The feast or famine cycle. Things would go extremely well for a while, then suddenly would flip, and bottom out like the stock market crash. Later, I would begin to understand why these unstable patterns was so constant in my life. Previous and further chapters in this book elaborate further with this topic. But that was me <u>trying to be with women.</u> Trust me, I get it. When you're single and winning. Waking up to thirty-five unread messages from an abundance of beautiful ladies unwilling to participate in the "I'll text him once, then make him wait" game must be the life. I have nothing but respect and admiration for professional athletes or movie stars that's married and settled down. I can only imagine the stress from temptation constantly being sent nudes from unbelievingly beautiful women and the bombarding of ladies at the clubs and parties literally begging these men to take them home with them. I know every day they must hate their lives with a passion. That was a joke. Please excuse my sarcasm. Won't happen again. But for me, the traditional, nine-to-five, everyday guys. It would get tough at times. All the more to make the commitment move once the ideal woman is placed in your life. Supply verses demand. I guess that's the balance in life. Everybody has an opportunity to win. That's the single man's struggle. Women on the other hand, fortunately do not share that same demise. Even the girl you would never think to believe, is in the game dating and having her pick of the litter with men can surprise you. Women struggle with quality not quantity with men. Stressing the point that most women I've met were never single, just in-between men. When you really think about it, who's really single anyway? The Oxford Dictionary on google defines single as "unmarried" or "not involved in a stable sexual relationship". I call it a top five. Now the numbers could vary from woman to woman. Some have more, some have less. Women tend to have their number one guy. The one man they would be willing to eliminate all other contacts to be with long term. Say it's their main squeeze. Just like in a situationship, being with this certain man would provide them with the relationship or life that would believe to complete their lives. Those men are either never interested in them the same as the women are, or they never fully commit enough to where a woman would discontinue keeping her options open. Then, the number two or the B guy is involved. That's the man who is the boyfriend material and may even play boyfriend from time to time for the woman. All while the female is trying to manipulate her brain into believing she's fully over her number one guy. B guy is a pleasant distraction for a woman because without him, it would be a constant chase with her number one. And women don't like to run and chase, they're terribly out of shape in that department. Mainly because it's discouraged even enforced by other women that chasing a man is considered weak and unlady-like. I say to each its own. The process isn't as important as the end result. But the number two usually gets stringed along because once number one shows any interest towards the woman, bye bye for B guy. He usually stays around and accepts his role because the brief rendezvous, guy number two indulges in sex, attention, and time with her.

And it's a tremendous feeling of promise and hope, so he continues to make himself available, knowing full well the position he's allowed himself to be in. Sex is an immensely powerful drug. Especially, if it provides an amazing high. This, of course, is a direct benefit of being the number two guy on the top five roster. Who else do you believe knows this very well? You guessed it. There are three others to mention. Or maybe no need to. Any guy after that, C-3, D-4, E-5 and so on. All just players on the bench. Some get playing time, most never see the field. Trust me, I've been a bench player more than a few times, where I've received my annual "hey stranger" text every now and then. Phone calls asking if I was in a relationship or married yet. Just to see if I'm still on her team or she needs to make a trade or roster change with another potential guy. Hope and lack of better availability is a tough truth. Life and decision making are siblings who love and fight each other often. Everybody fights a fight sometime in life. That's the game. Beneficial for some, demoralizing for others. One main reason for such specific and strategic motives for women, is mostly in part by the internal see saw battles with being alone verses being lonely and the thin blurry line that divides the two. When a woman tells you she's single, that could mean she is either getting over someone from a previous relationship which presents its own challenges, especially if it did not end well and left a distaste for future loves. Or, she's having a time figuring out what direction she wants to lean towards which guy she feels the most comfortable with. It's simply too easy and convenient for women to get men and it being they're not as hung up on looks and body types as much as their male counterparts, it makes it a simple add and subtract process for ladies to weave through their individual love lives. If you're lucky enough to be informed about your involvement in a particular females love octagon, consider it a privilege. At least then, you have an early option to either play your hand and try to win the pot or fold and take your losses elsewhere, giving another woman with a much smaller amount of poker players your undivided time and attention.

The only woman that actually informs you about where you stand in their love game is usually the one with the confidence and experience knowing other men after losing you is as easy to obtain as a great deal during black Friday. It's a simple plug and play. The hotter the female, the more disposable the men become. Only men with true leverage providing wants, cement their high place on the totem pole. Rough game I know. Just for a moment, allow yourselves in these women's high heels. Let's say, as a man, you could get any woman's phone number and call them, to which they would come to your house whenever you wanted. How would you determine which female was genuine and girlfriend material if you were looking for something unique and special? It's tough to find a fish in a lake full of ducks. Women may have options they entertain on a regular basis, even may sleep with different men at that time. Remember I said before, women give sex for love. Women also give sex for gifts, attention, security, materialistic items, food, I've seen and heard it all. And even through all that, these women still crave commitment. Women want a somebody not just somebodies. The game they play of relationship Plinko gets old and weary fast. Some see it as a necessity to find the right guy while not having any guy. Other women are more fortunate and come across the right one for them much earlier. Saving them the work and emotional erosion in the meantime creates. Regardless of the fact of how a woman goes about her life and finding her mate and the process that dictates it, that still serves no warrant to how a man acts towards her decision. I've been every option you can name for a female. The gas money guy, the flop house guy, the number one, two, three, four, and five. The last resort, the booty buddy. So on and so forth. All by choice of course. And I can honestly testify that if you don't enjoy yourself in that position when you get what you want, then you'll become extremely irate and tired when you don't. Women feel they've settled when they're tired of playing the game or heard enough horror stories to no longer participate. It just becomes us as men to make decisions whether to accept women as they are once, they come to that certain state of mind. The one thing I've seen women have the most trouble with accepting is taking responsibility for their lives and views on love being shaped and formed, due to choices they've consciously made on their own. As far as I'm concerned nothing begins romantically without a woman's consent. No texts, no phone calls, no messages on social media, no nothing. True, in order to grow the most, you must experience life through certain paths life provides you with. Some paths provide less obstacles and challenges than others. Who and what we choose is our choice and we must accept and make do with those choices the best we know how.

A Thought

I always was told that it was fine for a female to have random uncommitted sex with men like men do with women, but I believe that causes unhealthy habits with connecting with men in the future. We are creatures of habit. So, if a woman builds every experience with a man initiated through sex, when she finally decides to pursue a relationship with a man, how will she know how to connect other than through sex? Can you never exercise and then one day choose to join a gym, then just go right into a muscle building routine? The female is familiar with sex, so that's her initial investment. Men are pushed into alternative means of connections with women because sex isn't always a lay-up. Sometimes it takes other means of communication and connection with a woman to get her where they want to be. But for women, it's nothing to have sex. So, there's no other practices in order to connect, so when it's time to connect with a man and sex isn't suffice, the opportunity passes because those women possess no other means to entice a man to even consider a relationship because their go to, which is sex, simply becomes an opening magic trick.

XII.

Sweet Nothings

People ask me what my favorite song is. In the moment, I'll realize how difficult of a question that is. I have many favorite songs, all for various occasions. My favorite song for when I need inspiration is OutKast featuring Slick Rick, "The Art of Storytelling Pt. 1." My happy mood song is pretty much anything off Kayne West's *Graduation* album. And when I'm in any type of slump whether it be a writing or emotional one, for some reason Madonna's "Holiday" gets me going. Each piece of music that you listen to, plays an impactful part in one's life. It can be motivation for the day, peace for the night. I do have this unexplainable connection to the song "Sweet Love" by Anita Baker. It's easy to understand why the song is such a great listen and can bring someone's emotions out and front and center. I've heard of Anita Baker due to eavesdropping on conversations my parents had regarding her a few times, but never actually took the time to give a real listen for myself.

So, this one fateful day I was on YouTube scrolling and saw this video channel titled "Smooth Songs of the 80s". I clicked the channel and the very first song that came up was the "Sweet Love" song. As soon as the first few notes of the music began playing, I instantly recognized the song due to the artist Drake's track "Think Good Thoughts" which sampled this particular Anita Baker record. So, I believed that this song must be good if it was sampled by one of the most premiere artists of our day. As the sensual vocals of Anita began to rise through my speakers, I started feeling this amazing sense of calm and relaxation, like the feeling you get when you're standing under the shower head as the hot water hits your body after a tough rewarding workout. My mind instantly drifted to my happy place. Cascading goosebumps through my arms, giving me the internal tranquility I'd been longing for the entire day.

As soon as I completely submerged myself in the music, laying back, accepting my happiness, the heavenly angelic song ended, and I was brought back to consciousness, creating an instant thirst for another round of that former feeling. I may have listened to that song another nineteen times that day, each time feeling the same joy and warm bliss as if it were the first time I ever heard it. During the last time I was listening to that incredible song, vibing and being more in tune with the music, feeling as though I was swimming in the song. My phone rang and, in an instant, my peace and good feelings were quickly evaporated and shifted gears to sadness and unfulfillment. Even though on the other end of the phone was a friend whose calls I welcomed with open arms regularly. Just at this moment, I had a fever. And the only remedy was more cowbell. And my cowbell was Anita Baker's "Sweet Love".

That time in my life reminds me of a multitude number of experiences where I was blessed with that tremendous feeling then after a while, it ended. Over. Poof. Gone. Leaving me with an unpleasant feeling of loneliness, sadness, even some anger due to complete unawareness of exactly how quickly I could switch emotions and longing for that joy to return. See, I was not in control of my own destiny regarding the situations involving certain women. I see in most cases involving couples and staying power, is that for men and women to stay together long term, **the man has to be more into the woman than the woman is into the man.** That, for the most part, I tend to believe as truth. But, in many cases with how I dealt with females I was extremely interested in, that idea couldn't have back-fired more. Yes, the man must be emotionally invested vastly in his woman, but if she's not even slightly interested in the man, consider that relationship to be completely one-sided. I know the easiest response to a situation involving a man who's into a woman, while the woman isn't even the slightest interested in him to be an easy early exit stage left circumstance. But, what if you didn't know or was led to believe the woman was into you, when she actually was not? I'm not a dummy. Not by a long shot. Especially when it comes to understanding intent and reasoning behind people choosing to do certain things in life.

For most circumstances, I tend to rely on my logic. I think through the process and evaluate the best possible plan of action. That only pertains to everything else in life, but the woman I'm crazy about. For some unusual form of my anatomic makeup, my brain can put together reasonable ways to manage myself in regard to the fairer sex I'm not interested in. If she's not all that to me, I can refrain from acceptable amounts of attention and love distributed out for her. I can even go as completely dodging her presence all together. See, it's not just that I don't like the lady enough to want to give her my time. It's just that there's no incentive to pursue. I can see long term companionship with a woman rather quicky and if there's blank space available in my life bubble. I also can tune out my thoughts and cancel off the woman as an option. No matter how strong and aggressive her attempts to prove to me otherwise.

Unfortunately, when it comes to the women I desire and want, that logic and prime decision making I take so much pride in possessing, is suddenly kicked out of the window. Relationship hype and cloud nine feelings take place, allowing heartbreak and games of chase to fly in. I'll admit it. I crave the good feelings, the goosebumps down the arm, toe curling, smile from ear to ear, sweaty palm episodes when it involves a woman. It's the high I love to have. I hate to have to leave. Do you want to know who else understands that about me as well? What is the woman, Alex? Correct. I would meet a girl who physically stacks up to my liking. Pun intended. And I'm automatically hooked like a fish. That's all it would take initially. I become hers to lose. Now, I normally react well towards the females that I would be interested in and wouldn't entertain my intent further than their phone numbers, which they wouldn't answer any phone calls or any texts messages back. That would only break the spell they initially had over me. Causing me to lose interest after about a week or so, or even sometimes, I would substitute their intimacy status from the girlfriend box to the booty box, which I referred to in another chapter. On the other hand, if she opens the door, just enough by texting or messaging me back regularly, or answering the majority of my phone calls or even spending face to face time with me, kick the stick from under the box. Consider me got. It would be that simple. This mentality would actively dictate my ability to reason. You like me, I love you. You show me love; I give you the world. One plus one would equal a million in my heart mathematics book. So, why would I think otherwise if the stars are aligning from her side? I would get all these caring, loving, I miss you, hey bae messages from the woman I was interested in. Followed by the regular "come see me, wya?" phone calls.

Initially, it all just seemed as though I was rolling towards an amazingly brand-new relationship with a woman that I hoped and wished for. In retrospect, if the logical thinking side of my brain were intact and wasn't washed out by a tsunami of lust, mixed with butterfly like emotions, I could have seen the cracks in the perfect relationship scenario foundation earlier. For one, yes, in the beginning I would get plenty of messages in the morning from the woman telling me everything I wanted to hear from her. That would be followed by either a bad case scenario she was going through, or a want that was exposed like a need. Right after the morning, "hey baby" text and my resentful full sentence response, almost like clockwork, **the**

game would start. Initially, when I first would talk to a lady that showed interest, it was all friendly conversation, about how much she liked me, how great of a guy she thought I was, blah, blah, blah, and so on. The asking for things wouldn't really take place until about a week in. But once the first request was accepted, all hands-on deck. The first time a woman would ask for things, it would be minute things. Easily passed off as things she could get and do for herself. She would just seemingly inconvenience at the time. "Could I borrow some money? I get paid next week." Or the popular, "Wyd, in a little while? Wanna get some lunch? I'm starving."

Remember, looking back on that now, yes, I could have probably been more attentive towards the red flags a little earlier. And maybe that would have allowed me to align with the smarter side of managing those situations in a more proper fashion. I.E., kick those girls to the curb. Alas, me being the guy addicted to being immersed in the feeling of being needed and wanted by the women that made me think very improper thoughts, just from seeing them walk out of a gas station or jogging in the park.

I would tend to be oblivious to the fact. I was doing a Forrest gump run to their house, money in hand or restaurant reservations attached to a coupon app on deck. I mean, I still have to save a dollar when I can. It's just practical. This is where it would tend to get tricky. Remember before, how I mentioned women's options? Well, women also do a poor job of keeping men in the loop of their positions, as stand in guys or men waiting in the wind. This is a key component regarding to how women would determine a potential guy's positioning during his initial interview. If it just involves a meet and greet with a man being present to see the lady just to give her some money. She won't go to great lengths to keep her phone away or even to turn it off when she was around you. However, her story to why she can't be with a man any more than just a few minutes before she had to leave and go back inside, without your continued company or leave because of that thing she had forgotten to do, is already prepared and ready to execute. High chances are I'm not the first guy she's entertained like this and can place sure bets I'm not the last.

So, her level of seasoning at that point is veteran. If a woman knows what she's doing, she can take from you, without you feeling taken. Promises of more time and one on one encounters can persist once she feels that man can become a dependable source of income and other useful resources. It's the chase for more of her that would drive me towards a more materialistic persuasion in hopes of one day winning the race. That race ran too often, and was designed for a no-win contest. I was thinking I'd get a leg up, in order to one day get a particular girl. All I became was a step ladder for a woman to reach the goal or guy for which she was truly aiming. The reason that getting involved in a situation like this can become so painful isn't the time and resources a man spends convincing a female she's better off with him and then she is telling him it was all a façade. But rather, after she tells a man her true intentions for him and then he now works to convince her games are no longer necessary. Then asking for a true shot at love. Making him now even more committed in making the female his girl legitimately. All that does is show a woman that his commitment is a welcome mat to maximize her opportunity for getting all she can from him without any regret or remorse. A simple case of **fear of loss versus hope for gain**. If the woman feels that losing that particular man has no negative effect on her grand scheme of getting what she wants out of life, then she will behave accordingly. If she feels that keeping that man will ultimately help her cause however, same rules apply. I've been in a situation where a girl told me the truth that she just used me to buy her stuff but then said she actually liked me and now wanted to pursue a legitimate relationship with me. She even went as far as asking for fairness and if she could take me out to eat. To which, I would like to add, I would never turn down a satisfying meal, especially from a woman I was interested in, but I digress. Imagine the confusion and wild sense of excitement I was feeling once she told me that. My initial thought was, this is what I put all this time and energy into. Finally, my arduous work paid off and I was being rewarded or, so I believed. The other side of my thinking, however, began to slap itself into real awareness. She didn't want a relationship; she was in that quick moment of remorse for her actions and seeking reconciliation. Still, she didn't want to lose my financial backing so she figured she could keep me in her life by a false version of a relationship, to which the next day, she confessed to me as well. Security tends to bring out the truth in people. I think she just started going to church and that pastor must have given a lesson on taking advantage or to grab every apple you can or something. Either way, the lessons I've learned from those types of experiences are valued today and greatly appreciated. I couldn't have really faulted those ladies that tried to get what they wanted from me. I mean for the most part; I didn't walk away empty handed, either. There were times I received my share, as well. Even if only for small moments that were spaces far and in-between. I see now, that a true relationship isn't forced. It isn't something that should feel like a one-way street. Due to the fact of past events and experiences women grab and squeeze on to, it's normal to feel some kind of resisting or even weariness when it comes to females leaning toward giving men chances. I was told that **the older a woman gets, the more stuff gets in the way.** The way a person treats you is usually a direct reaction to how they were treated. Hurt people can hurt people even if the intent isn't there. Regardless of that mentality, as a man, you shouldn't feel like the chase is a long hard road with a pot of gold on the other side of a dark lagoon. It should feel like a fulfilling journey, chock-full of joyous moments and gems of growth, encouragement to continue the road with no signs of stopping because of cautious feelings.

No, I can't give you an example of a proper road to love. I grew up in a successful two parent home with plenty of love. But even that example is no blueprint. There're many different successful stories that may seem more relatable. There's nothing wrong with taking care of Your Woman. In fact, I encourage it. Gift your girl up. As long as it feels like a return instead of a withdrawal, you'll never lose that good feeling that put you in the race in the first place.

XIII.

Been There, Done That

Things happen in life. I get that. I really do. The most complicated events during a person's time on this earth, I believe, is effort towards living unfortunate life free. We all make mistakes. We all achieve great moments of shortcoming. The question is not what the poor choices are however, but more towards the line of how those decisions dictate the "these" decisions we have yet to make. See, I'm no slouch in the kitchen. On a scale of ordering pizza to being Bobby Flay, I see myself vaulting to at least the second round in the TV show "Who Can Cook the Only Four Dishes They Know the Best?" Because I know this, I tried cooking for a few female compadres just to see how far that would get me. You understand the saying, "The way to a man's heart is through his stomach." Try cooking your undeniable signature dish for a female and watch what body parts of hers she starts introducing you to first. All I'm saying is that ladies love lunch. I know this because I tried this with an overwhelmingly high success rate. Cooking for a date became a back pocket go-to, which is why meeting an incredibly beautiful female at WalMart with my shopping cart full of items fit for a candlelight feast for two entitled me to converse with her. The setting was ideal for a romantic comedy. I'm at the self-checkout, she's at the self-checkout. I'm dressed to impress and she's a woman. I'm already impressed. To make a short story even shorter, we talk, exchange numbers and part ways. I got home, started cooking and decided to send that girl a text, asking if she would like to see the reason why I bought all that good food, since she was staring at my groceries so hard. Always ready to exert my back pocket go-to. It's a shot in the proverbial dark, I know. A true fifty-fifty shot she takes me up on my offer, hopefully based off my first impression would be enough to entice this young lady for a comfortable home cooked meal. Topped with good laughs and strong connection. Or, I get the cops called on me for attempted kidnapping. I know women have watched enough ID Channel and read enough magazines to know it's a risk to be at someone's house you just met. On the contrary, I can name times on both hands and feet where women have told me meeting a guy off a dating website at their house was as common as driving without a seatbelt on. Like I said, a fifty-fifty shot. That's not why this story is significant.

What begins my point was her response, "Yeah, no I don't go by a man's house that I don't know anymore." Not never, not won't, not can't.

She said, "anymore". The way a woman's brain can store a memory of a favorable experience with a man, the exact could be said about an unfavorable one. When a moment goes bad, it prompts us as human beings to store that information to use as a decision barrier, to not repeat that event again in life. Not because of what went wrong, but because of what didn't go right. I'm a why guy. Sometimes I can't help myself. I believe things and people don't just become A then Z without passing A through Y first. Which sparked my question in response to this cautious woman's reply. I simply asked her, why didn't she house date after meeting someone anymore?

What I received was a "It's a long story."

Wrong answer. Open discussion is my game and I have nothing but time. From our honest conversation, what I came to discover wasn't that this lady suffered any abuse or trauma from her encounters at these men's homes, but rather disappointment and consistent loss of power and control of the direction of the relationships at the hands of mastered seduction and empty promises. She went to these men's places looking to establish, or if nothing else push forward strong solid long-term relationships but just ended up gathering girlfriend pink slips and expired "good morning beautiful" text messages. See, if a woman is in a situation to where things didn't go as she planned but it was of no consequence to her because no investments or expectations were initiated, then no issues fester. No harm, no foul. But once desire and want gets included, then she's denied, unhappiness takes center stage in her mind. Not to mention the memory bricks that start to build up and block that choice. Females will tend to associate those decisions with failure and ultimately talk herself out of that option, thinking it protects her, which then allows her to feel good. It's all about outcome. The end result. If sex on the first night leads to no more phone calls from the guy she liked. The end result, she no longer has sex on the first night. At that moment, first night sex equals single life. So, she adds a memory brick to that decision. It does not mean she won't ever have sex on the first encounter with a man again. It just means if and when that opportunity presents itself again, she just expects a negative outcome. So, in most instances, she will stop talking to the guy before he ever could gain the choice to quit her first. Negative mindsets don't just stem from unfulfilled experiences with men. Women can latch on to any event in their life to use as marked moments to influence their future decision making.

The body has a natural process of building immunity towards certain diseases, but only after it has been exposed to them. Women react the same way. They protect themselves from hurt and loss with defense mechanisms. But, that's due to exposure from the hurt and pain. The hesitations, fear, resistance and quickness to desert, all stem from previous experiences where they did not initially act that way but now do.

I was cool with a woman who told me a time she wore pants to a birthday party that were just way too tight, but they fit her just right, she said. She reached down to tie her shoes and heard a rip that stopped the music, stopped the party, and turned the necks of every single person at that party in her ripped pants direction. To which, she told me she stood up, shifted her hair to one side and promptly walked out of the party, got in her car, and drove straight home. Now, was that a little extreme? Of course. Especially, since she told me no one really laughed. Most chased after her, offering assistance they could support and comfort her. Not to mention the body this queen had, ripping any piece of clothing to reveal her troublemaker panties. (Her words not mine) Would be a present and blessing in itself. No need for a birthday party.

Nonetheless, it's not always the what that happens to us. It's all about how we see it as it's unfolding. My perspective from her eyewitness account looked like an opportunity for a good laugh for everyone, my homegirl included, and a great ice breaker to reference for future barbeques and other social gatherings. But what she took from her experience was a twenty to thirty second nightmare and lightning bolt of embarrassment with shame. A real live horror movie if you let her tell it. Persuading her to not only shy away from pants that are too tight, but to give up on the attire completely. That's right. Since that moment, her wardrobe consisted of leggings and sundresses. This woman looks at a pair of jeans like I look at a poisonous snake, with sheer terror and world ending panic. Yes, again I notice this is a rare example of cause and effect, but the aftermath is all relative. If the perceived hurt isn't followed up by an equal amount of reward, then the hurt is the only factor from the memory that's left. Every situation may not always end up so one sided for women who experienced these events however, there can be situations to where a woman might have felt pain, but still possessed enough good to latch on to believe something or someone is worth pursuing. You might not be a Superbowl champion but, winning your division and hosting a playoff game sure is a momentum builder for next season. Just allow enough sugar with the salt and the moment becomes bearable. I've seen a woman left at a restaurant table while the guy slipped out the back door, then seen weeks later with the same guy at the movie theater. Encounters like those could potentially end up burning bridges for these women with men, sometimes permanently. Building enough memory bricks to create emotional fortresses no amount of game or charm could penetrate. It's just as much the time as it is the action that can change a woman's perspective to words what she will and won't give to a man. **Time heals all wounds and also <u>reveals</u> all wounds.** If a female's initial investment in someone seems to be moving forward towards something concrete, then she sees that as investing time. If the movement feels stationary or in the backwards direction, then she's wasting it. If a woman cuts her finger putting on a dress but then takes a picture that gets a thousand likes on social media, it's considered a victory. No likes, then all she received was a bloody finger. Then, women that I have met at one point in their lives have been a lot more open-minded. If something seemed like a promising idea, sure. A benefit dangled at the end of a string, let's do it. The only unfortunate part of trial and error was the error part. The mindset then sways from receptive to protective. That's how the stages of the process of elimination take shape. It's not that a woman doesn't want to do or go along with certain things, it's just she feels as though she can't any longer.

Fear - an unpleasant often strong emotion caused by the belief that someone or something is dangerous, likely to cause pain, or a threat.

Doubt - uncertainty or belief or opinion that often interferes with decision making. A deliberate suspension of judgement.

Fear is powerful. I hear the term "overcome your fears" all the time. Sources from television to the internet, to everyday people preaching fear as a mountain to climb. Once conquered, the world becomes at your fingertips, from the mighty strength you now possess from its defeat. Fear is a challenge yes, but an action word encouraged to do so. Fear is caution but not immobility. I know fearful women who still gives relationships and love the ole college try. Sure, it takes considerable time but if the partner they choose turns out to be in their favor, fear subsides, hope forms and optimism becomes the leading thought.

Doubt, however, is a much more menacing monster to denounce. Doubt can give a female enough bad energy to not only lean towards not taking a chance, but she also forfeits her ability to even consider weighing her options. Her doubtful mind reminds her of the previous three times she gave love a chance. All three times, initial investment. All three times, no real return. This mental ball and chain capture will take place before you, as a man, can even text and simply invite her to accompany you for a simple cup of coffee. The opportunity is already dead, and you didn't even see it coming. She convinces herself, why bother? And that statement alone becomes the single women's battle cry. For women I've met that didn't allow doubt to paralyze their steps, doubt simply shifted their plan of action. Their dating life, sex life and overall interactions with men became a running shot clock with no timeouts, or even a whistle to blow, stopping the play.

Having to EARN a Woman's Trust

The reason a woman doesn't just trust a man from the jump in a relationship, is due to a full investment of trust in a former or first relationship that ended in failure. It's forward hope and promise with wrongdoing and unfulfilled circumstance taken away. Her present becomes her future minus her past. (P=F-Pt)

It's how long a female deals with them, can remove and replace a man on her terms, that creates control. That control protects her feelings which never fully gets involved, which in turn creates comfort. That comfort creates a false sense of security which develops inconsistent dealings with men. That in turn, raises even more doubt. That doubt eradicates any opportunity for a long-term relationship. A relationship where a consistent, healthy, solid bond with a man could remove the doubt entirely. Sunrise, sunset. And just like that, the window closes. It's a cycle, a Ferris wheel cycle. Where the attitude during the interaction won't change, but the men in her life will. It's like a baseball player constantly changing his glove because he can never catch a pop fly ball, but the reason is because every time the sun gets in his eyes, he misses the catch. So, the player pretends to be sick during day games. It's built-up frustration and that energy carries for as long as a female feels that way. Even if the game is at night, the outfielder will still find a problem in the lights, so when another ball is dropped, he'll just buy another glove because finding a fix is easier on the ego than finding the source. Especially when the source is that person.

I knew a woman who I nicknamed "Nah" because she said no to everything.

You wanna go out?

"Nah."

It's reggae night at the club.

"Nah."

Drake concert tickets, front row?

"Nah."

Didn't wanna do anything with any man ever. She even tried dating another woman at one time. She broke up with her because she had guy friends. Yes, it was that serious. If an action reminded her of a past man mishap, then no need to put on that swimsuit. She wasn't even going to touch that water. In life, you grow and learn or you don't. Some pain you simply can't scratch out. You must erase to eliminate entirely. A woman can see events as what was and what ifs. Neither thoughts men influence. Presenting a what can be, is best case scenario. Whether or not that dish gets served or not is entirely up to that woman's appetite for that day.

Metamorphosis- The Three Stages of the "Modern Woman"

1.) "Caterpillar" stage - When a female is young and identifies herself through her actions and experiences throughout her young life. She grows and dates, has sexual experiences, relationships, and moments that tend to shape her life, children, unsuccessful relations/situations with men, and tries that come to no avail. Negative consequences result in negative mindsets.

2.) "Cocoon" stage - The moment that young woman, after her failed attempts in her love life, begins to isolate herself and shelter in place emotionally and psychologically regarding men. She builds walls to keep from connecting from men and starts to assume there's either no reason to connect or a dire consequence to connecting with men will ensue.

3.) "Butterfly" stage - The transformation to where a woman will begin to open up and try exploring options again, due to the want and need to have a companion. Will tend to have a more positive approach towards men and pursue the natural goals and biological desires a woman possesses during her life from birth like marriage and family.

XIV.

You REALLY Wanna Know Why I Wrote This Book?

It only took me a few months to write this book. I'm serious. I started the first chapter which was "Why did I even write this book?" around March and by the end of May, all but a few final pieces here and there remained. To be completely honest, sometimes I do question myself to why I decided to write the book. Yes, I understand in the prelude, I gave you legitimate reasoning to what motivated me to document "the Woman in the Middle." It was my release therapy for remembering a time when I felt the most sure and unsure about myself in my entire life. My confidence level is sort of how momentum sways back and forth in sports. In basketball, let's say a team is down twenty-five points with eight minutes left in the third quarter. The entire game for this team has been relatively the same. There were missed shots and then some made ones. Just like a normal game would transpire. But then something would just turn with how this particular team would shoot the basketball at the end of the quarter. With eight full minutes left, every shot for this team would go in. Seventeen for seventeen shooting with five of those shots being three pointers. So, now instead of the team walking with their heads down into the fourth quarter, they now are high fiving and flexing into the next period with an almost forty-point swing, now putting them up with an entire quarter left to play. One minute, their team couldn't buy a bucket, the next their putting the opposing team in ICU mode. That's how I typically manage my life situations. If I'm down, I'm down. I'll begin to feel doubtful, but all I will need is a few things start to work in my favor and the light and the end of the tunnel brightens. Optimism on full blast. During my debating phase, where I was contemplating on if I should write the book or not, I was in the middle of reading another book called *Who Says You Can't, You Do* by Daniel Chidiac. It was the best investment I ever put into myself. It was a tremendous self-help book I recommend to anybody looking for clarity into why their lives just don't make any sense. I applied the teachings to my own life, and it definitely allowed me to make the right decision to start and complete the book. I was going through a time where I was angry and frustrated. Angry with how my life was unfolding, but how I couldn't see what directions I could have taken that could have u-turned and placed my life on a more fluid and rewarding road. Providing me with more purpose and less disappointing outcomes. Wondering, if I had lived in various places, possessed different fields of work, or even changed my physical form, would my life been more purposeful? Maybe so. Maybe not. But the life experiences would have been different, and I might not have been able to construct the book the way it came out. Life is important to keep living because being able to look back at the lessons learned later on is the real gift. I thought of the way my life unfolded and played those scenarios in my head repeatedly like a DVD movie set to repeat. I realized quicky, that brought nothing but poor sleeping habits, constant negative thoughts, and the inability of how amazing and blessed my life actually was and continues to be. I can see clearly now. If my life was been different and more of what I always constructed in my head, would I have learned what I did about Love and life? Men and women co-existing in this label heavy, materialistic, nontraditional world. Who knows? What I do know is, I have my life. Which is designed for a very dynamic viable purpose. Sometimes, I must remind myself of that. Everything being said in this segment of the book is necessary because during my dealings with women and the amazing and then sometimes not so amazing outcomes that would take place, I had questions. Those results sometimes took on how I once viewed relationships and how they should have been formed. I had just as many failed attempts at the type of women I wanted as the Wright brothers and their pursuits of owning the blue skies. The more I went, the more was spent. Energy, time, resources, you name it. The saying goes, "pressure makes diamonds". Well, here's my shiny new book. Hope you enjoyed it. My dating life was pressure, filled with wonder and knowledge. I was processing millions of questions in my head, trying to piece together events in my life. Such as, "What can I say or not say to make this girl happen in my life?"

Am I too focused on the movie romance instead of pursuing an actual relationship? I admit, my parent's relationship growing up influenced me. How Will Smith pursued Eva Mendes in the movie *Hitch* inspired me. The way Mike loved Alicia in *The Wood* moved me. And the way John and Laurie understood each other in *Ted* gave me hope that I could be myself and still be able to find my match. These few examples kept the fire burning in my quest for companionship. Although the journey seemed too long and trying at times, my eyes remained on the prize. I learned it's not about how many times you go through obstacles and challenges in your life, it's the attitude you take on once you continue confronting them.

Watching videos on the internet one day, I viewed two separate women's one-hundred-meter hurdle events back-to-back. One video highlighted a young lady running the event about as poorly as you can imagine. She hit and knocked down about every hurdle in the race and about halfway through, she just ceased to continue jumping over the remaining hurdles and just barged through them. That competition became a monster truck rally, with this runner just creating a massive track of knocked down and damaged hurtles with the runner not even fully completing the race. At first glance, it was a hilarious video and could easily have been put on the show

Ridiculousness. But then, after digging a little deeper into the video and seeing how I could apply that visual towards my own life, I seen that this runner believed that when in doubt, just crash into things. She didn't improve one bit on being a better runner and hurdler.

When I scrolled to the next video however, it revealed the same outcome but displayed a different lesson. This hurdler started out the blocks with much more power and explosiveness than the runner on the previous video. Her running and technique must have shaped her fate in that race. The very first hurdle tripped the runner and she stumbled and fell right to the track. Of course, once an event such as that occurs, the race is finished for a runner, such as that. But what occurred next inspired me to include this example in the book. The runner gathered herself, stood up, backed up a few steps and raced for the hurdle. Which she cleared. Then, when attempting the next hurdle again, she trips and falls. To which, she repeated the same steps as before. Get up, backed up, and raced for the hurdle, which she completed by leaping over with not even a bump involving the obstacle. She cleared every hurdle after that until she reached the end of the race. At the end of the video, I absorbed the mentality behind the hurdler's dedication to finishing the race the way she did. Her mission was to complete the race, not just to finish. No matter the difficulty or the magnitude of adversity that stood between the race and the finish line, those hurdles would be leaped over, and the race would be completed. Along the way, because the runner took her time with making sure she worked her technique and jumped every hurdle instead of just running through them like the previous runner demonstrated. She grew in that moment as a better racer, so the next time she participates in, she will have the knowledge and experience that the race can be completed in a well structured efficient manner.

I know it doesn't make sense, sometimes, to keep going through things, especially with the high failure rate I was facing. But, I knew what I wanted or at least believed I did. Overall, I desire love just like everyone else. To feel special and be valued in a way that's deserving of how I treat myself. I feel Ima relationship guy. The kind that does better with that special someone instead of without. However, I am also like anyone else who travels through life and love on a constant teeter totter of indecision and confusion. Somedays, I'm in the mood to become a taken man removed from the market and then other days, I welcome the concept of just enjoying my life being a bachelor. Living life, not having to find out the true intentions of women I'm with in the moment and accepting certain consequences as they come along. That's me. I think a lot. I grew up in a household where two people respected and loved each other through the best and worst of times. It's those young memories that inject me with hope and also heartburn towards pursuing that kind of connection. This book was not just about figuring out women. The book was not just an attempt to crack the code on a women's mentality in the new age world we live in today. It is just a simple form of creating awareness towards the why with females' decision-making regarding dating and relationships. The sabotaging of those relationships, to the mindset of mending them back together.

Like I said in the beginning of the book, I'm sure there's a percentage of women who connect themselves to the chapters in the book, while there's others who read the book with confusion because their experiences may not match with what they have read. To that I say, just keep on living. It's amazing the mentality changes from eighteen to thirty-eight. Those twenty years are something serious. I say to every able-bodied man reading this, thank you. This book was many years in the making, and you taking time out of your tough, stressful, man-filled day to read my words is the most rewarding feeling I can have in my life thus far. It's one man's story told but I'm sure it's a story many men have heard. Tell your story. I'm sure it's one exciting tale not yet told. Remember, **"Life's a takeoff and a landing, just try to enjoy the flight."** It's not about what people tell you that is important. It's how you receive it that matters. I didn't take the smoothest path traveled to get here, but you saw what I did with my half full glass of water. In the end, it's all about cause and effect. So, you just finished the book. Now what?